eat this with...
Paso Robles Wine 2

by Lisa Pretty

Paso Robles is the perfect place to plan a wine tasting adventure with a picnic break along the way. Many of the Paso wineries offer picnic facilities so that their guests may relax and enjoy the surrounding beauty. One of my favorite picnic stops is at Pear Valley. The tasting room is surrounded by several picnic locations with views of the vineyards. The sound of water trickling from the fountain, along with music piped through the air help visitors relax as they sip their wine and enjoy the company of friends both old and new.

Pretty Media Creations
179 Niblick Road #102
Paso Robles, CA 93446

ISBN-978-1-62407-562-9

EatThisWith.com

foreward

The first "eat this with...Paso Robles Wine" recipe book was published in 2011. I created that book as a way of sharing many of my recipes that I enjoyed paired with Paso Robles wine.

The Paso Robles wineries were all very supportive of my project, with 38 wineries offering the book for sale in their tasting room. Several people asked when the next book would arrive. So, I decided to do a second and include additional Paso wine pairings.

To make this book even more of a tribute to Paso Robles, I decided to get the local chefs involved in the project. As a result you will find a wide range of recipes from some of Paso Robles' top chefs who represent local restaurants and catering businesses.

Chapter 7 was one of my favorites to create. In this chapter you will find several complete wine friendly menus.

Most wineries paired up with local chefs to produce spectacular menus that the home cook could replicate when entertaining guests. Others decided this was a great opportunity to share some of their special recipes that they have made for winemaker dinners, club events or as a special meal for guests. The recipes for items included in the menus can be found in the earlier chapters.

There are really no hard and fast rules for pairing wine with food. In the first book I did introduce some of the basic guidelines for a successful pairing. If the wine and food taste good together to you, then it is a winning combination. Don't be intimidated, just experiment and find ones you enjoy!

contents

salads - 59

butter leaf - 61
tomato salad - 62
greek salad - 63
caesar salad - 65
salad lyonnaise - 67
super salad - 69
tabbouleh salad - 70
barley salad - 71
mixed shellfish and couscous salad - 73
field mache with shitake bacon - 75
nicoise - 77
insalata alle-pia - 78
wasabi salmon -79

soups - 81

chilled pea soup - 82
gazpacho - 83
vichyssoise - 85
purée of fagioli bean soup - 87
minestrone - 88
french onion soup - 89
hearty potato soup - 90
oyster saffron chowder - 91
sweet potato soup - 92
black bean soup - 93

entrées - 95

prosciutto wrapped swordfish - 97
fish potato casserole - 98
grilled halibut - 99
curry tilapia - 101
grilled game hens provencal - 102
chicken saltimbocca - 104
chicken kiev - 106
herb roasted chicken - 109
chicken vindaloo - 111
chicken briani - 113
italian sausage and beans - 114
grilled duck breast - 115
pan roasted duck breast - 116
turkey loaf - 118
kevin's mac & cheese - 119
andy's sauerkraut - 121
dusi stew and polenta - 122
paella with kalua pork - 125
tenderloin of pork - 127
pork kebabs - 128
teriyaki flank steak - 129
crown roast - 131
pork puttanesca - 133
stuffed rolled pork - 135
mutton curry - 137
game meat pie - 138

grilled lamb chops - 141
lamb orecchiette - 142
leg of lamb - 144
braised lamb shank - 145
grilled strip lion - 146
tri tip with salsa - 148
skirt steak roule - 149
pan roasted ribeye - 150
braised short ribs - 153
braised short ribs with polenta - 155

desserts - 157

grilled peaches - 159
baked plums - 160
blackberry clafoutis - 162
peach cobbler - 163
carrot halwa - 164
pavlova - 165
chocolate macadamia souffle - 166
dark chocolate profiteroles - 167
belgium chocolate mousse - 169
manchego cheesecake - 171
walnut carrot cake - 172
chocolate caramel tart - 175
mini pecan tarts - 177
smore's chocolate tart - 178
grandma's espresso chocolate brownies - 181
molten chocolate cakes - 183

menus - 185

Pairing Food and Wine

Just in case you did not read the first edition of this book, I am reprinting a few basic guidelines to help with pairing food and wine. There are some basic characteristics of a wine that will determine which food pairings will work.

Acidity: In general acidity is a good thing. Acidity enhances flavor and in the case of a wine will help it age. The acidity in wine will brighten the flavor of food and will cut through fat. On the other hand, an acidic wine will typically not go well with a creamy dish.

Body: Wines can be light, medium or very full bodied. For the most part you want to pair the body of the wine with the body of the food. For a creamy dish a nice round wine, for a light dish a fairly light, crisp wine. For a juicy steak a big wine usually wins. You get the idea, don't put a delicate white with a spicy rib.

Sweetness: When grapes are fermented the natural sugars in the grapes are converted to alcohol. When almost all of the sugar is converted the wine is considered dry. If some of the sugar is not converted that sugar is referred to as residual sugar. A wine can be off dry as is the case with many Rieslings, to very sweet as is typically found in a Late Harvest Zinfandel. There are times when pairing contrasting levels of sweetness in the food with the sweetness of a wine will work. One thing to be careful of is when it comes to dessert if your dessert is a lot sweeter than your wine it will make your wine seem bitter. Some people say the wine should always be sweeter than the dessert; however, I have found several pairings with the wow factor where that is not the case.

Tannins: While tannins are naturally occurring in wine and soften over time, young wines with lots of tannins will seem very astringent. If you have a tannic wine the best thing to do is serve it with a fatty meat with a bit of spice.

Oak: Oak flavors on both white and red wine can be very pleasant. It will clearly impact the pairing with food. Oaky whites tend to go well with creamy items or roasted foods. Oaky reds are great with grilled food and can hold up to spicy items.

How a food is prepared will also have a lot to do with which wine pairings will work.

Stir-frying: This cooking method is for a fast preparation that preserves the food's flavor and color. Although the type of fat, spice and sauce used will dictate the successful pairings, in general you will want to avoid oaky wines, will want a fairly acidic wine and likely a light to medium bodied wine. White or reds often work here.

Grilling: Grilling uses dry heat and seals all the juices in the meat or vegetable while often leaving a crusty surface. Typically, grilled food will have a smoky flavor making it match well with wines that have a fair amount of oak flavor. In general, full bodied red wines with tannins and bold fruit work well with grilled food. A medium to full bodied white that has been aged in oak can also work well.

Braising and Stewing: The idea of slow cooking in liquid is to soften the meat and provide deep flavors. Typically a fair amount of herbs and spices are used. For braised meats or stews go big. The typical cuts of meat will have some fat that can hold up to tannins and most herbs beg for a bold wine.

A final tip is if it is difficult to pair… pick a sparkling wine! There is hardly anything that doesn't pair with bubbles.

chapter 1 - appetizers

proscuitto wrapped peaches by Chef Alex Martin, Crush Catering

Proscuitto Wrapped Peaches with Blue Cheese, Red Wine Gastrique, Toasted Pepitas, Garden Pea Shoots

Yield

8 thin slices of prosciutto, halved length wise
2 medium peaches—halved, pitted and cut into
8 wedges each
Salt and freshly ground pepper
1 tablespoon olive oil
4 ounces of creamy blue cheese, crumbled
2 ounces of pea shoots
1 ounces fresh lemon juice
1/2 cup red wine (I used Shale Oak Zinfandel)
1/2 cup red wine vinegar
2/3 cup agave nectar
1 cup large raw pepitas (pumpkin seeds)
1 teaspoon olive oil
1-1/2 teaspoon ground coriander
3/4 teaspoon kosher salt
1/2 teaspoon dried dill
1/4 teaspoon freshly ground black pepper
Pinch cayenne (optional)

eat this with...
Eberle Barbera
Shale Oak Zinfandel
Doce Robles Barbera

- Lay the prosciutto slices out on a work surface. Set a peach wedge at the edge of each slice, season with salt and pepper and top with crumbled blue cheese. Roll up the prosciutto to enclose the peaches. Heat a grill over medium heat. Brush the peaches lightly with olive oil. Grill peaches turning occasionally, until the prosciutto is browned and crisp, about 4 minutes.

- To make the gastrique, place the agave nectar in a sauce pot and cook over medium heat until it turns dark amber in color, about 5 minutes. Add the red wine, vinegar and continue cooking until the mixture has reduced to a syrupy consistency, about 15 minutes. Season with salt to taste.

- For the toasted pepitas position a rack in the center of the oven and heat the oven to 325°F. Toss the seeds with the olive oil on a baking sheet large enough to hold them in a single layer. Spread in an even layer and roast the seeds in the oven, stirring occasionally, until golden, 13 to 15 minutes. Remove the pan from the oven and immediately toss the seeds with the coriander, salt, dill, pepper, and cayenne, if using. Let cool for 10 minutes.

- Cut pea shoots in half and place in a mixing bowl. Toss with olive oil, fresh lemon juice, salt.

smoked salmon dip by Simply Incredible

This dip is perfect for parties. Serve with raw vegetables, bread sticks, or flatbread crackers.

Yields 1 1/3 Cups

    8 ounces cream cheese or Neufchatel, softened
    ½ cup Greek yogurt, plain
    1 tablespoon fresh lemon juice
    2 tablespoons capers
    2 tablespoons finely chopped red onion
    2 tablespoons chopped fresh dill
    4 ounces smoked Alaskan wild salmon, coarsely chopped
    Lemon and lime slices for garnish (optional)

- Combine first six ingredients with a hand mixer or in a food processor and pulse until blended. Stir in salmon.

- Place dip in serving container. For an added touch, garnish with lemon and/or lime slices.

eat this with...

Clavo Cellars Sparkling
Clayhouse Estate Syrah
Eberle Chardonnay
Halter Ranch Rosé
Pear Valley Chardonnay
Penman Springs Rosé
Pomar Junction Merlot
Robert Hall Grenache
Summerwood Merlot

chapter 1 - appetizers

grilled figs by Ian McPhee, McPhee's Grill

When figs are in season, this grilled fresh figs stuffed with goat cheese wrapped in prosciutto is the appetizer to make. Just a little bit a prep work and a few minutes on the grill for a quick and easy appetizer.

Serves 4

8 fresh figs, cut in half top to bottom
4 ounces fresh goat cheese
8 slices prosciutto, see-through thin

- ❧ Stuff each fig half with goat cheese and wrap in prosciutto.
- ❧ Brush lightly with olive oil.
- ❧ Grill, cheese side down, for 2 minutes. Turn over grill for 4 minutes.

eat this with...

Ancient Peaks Rosé
Castoro Pinot Grigio
Derby Sparkling
J. Lohr Chardonnay
JUSTIN Rose
Niner Sangiovese
Pear Valley Frizzante
Robert Hall Grenache Blanc
Villa San Juliette Grenache Blanc

artichoke dip by Sarah Leslie

Sarah is often invited to parties and pot-luck events. This is her "go to" recipe
that delights guests every time. Serve this warm with artisan bread or sliced baguette.

Serves 12

2 cans artichoke hearts, drained and chopped

1 8-ounce package cream cheese

1 cup grated Parmesan

3/4 cup sour cream

3/4 cup mayonnaise

5 ounces fire roasted peppers (optional)

- Mix all ingredients and place in a 9 inch pie pan

- Bake at 325F for 35-40 minutes

eat this with...

Cass Grenache
Caliza Syrah
DAOU Chardonnay
Opolo Pinot Grigio
Pear Valley Aglianico
Pomar Chardonnay
Robert Hall Cabernet Sauvignon
Still Waters Cabernet Sauvignon
Summerwood Cabernet Sauvignon

chapter 1 - appetizers

yellow-pepper hummus by Brigit Binns

Making your own hummus is super-simple, and the payoff in flavor is substantial (another benefit: no preservatives or other chemical additives). Plus, you can adjust the spices to taste; why not up the garlic and cumin slightly for this sun-kissed Mediterranean snack platter.

Serves 6

Two (14-ounce) cans chickpeas, drain and reserve liquid
¾ teaspoon kosher salt
1/8 teaspoon cayenne pepper
1/3 cup tahini (sesame) paste
6 pitted calamata olives
1 ½ teaspoons minced garlic
½ teaspoon ground cumin
1/3 cup fresh lemon juice
1/3 cup extra-virgin olive oil, plus extra for drizzling
1 large roasted yellow pepper, cored, seeded, and cut into
¼-inch strips lengthwise
Garnish:
1 tablespoon chopped yellow pepper
1 tablespoon finely chopped flat-leaf parsley
1 tablespoon additional Extra Virgin Olive Oil

Drain the chickpeas well, reserving the juices. In a food processor, combine all the ingredients, except the olive oil. Add 2 tablespoons of the juice from the can, and pulse to a rough puree. With the motor running, add the olive oil slowly, process until slightly chunky and emulsified. (If the mixture is too stiff to move, add another tablespoon of the liquid from the can; not more—the mixture should hold its shape). Refrigerate, covered, for up to 48 hours if desired. To serve, remove from the refrigerator and mound into one or two bowls. Arrange the chopped yellow pepper on top of the hummus, drizzle with a little olive oil and scatter with the parsley.

eat this with...

Caliza Pink
Clavo Viognier
DAOU Chardonnay
Halter Ranch Syrah
Pear Valley Pinot Noir
Robert Hall Viognier
Shale Oak Zinfandel
Wild Horse Pinot Noir
Windward Pinot Noir

onion tarts by Lisa Pretty

There is nothing like sweet caramelized onions and pastry. The only thing that could make that better is a little pancetta!

These tarts can be made for tiny finger food versions or larger as a small plate served with a bed of dressed greens.

eat this with...

Asuncion Ridge Pinot Noir
Adalaida Viognier
Cass Viognier
Graveyard Tombstone Pink
Pear Valley Syrah
Robert Hall Viognier
Tablas Creek Rosé
Venteux Pinot Noir
Windward Pinot Noir

Yield

1 package puff pastry sheets, thawed in refrigerator overnight
Egg wash (1 egg beaten with 1 tablespoon water)
½ stick salted butter
3 large sweet onions, peeled and sliced
1 teaspoon dried sage
1 tablespoon brown sugar (optional)
1 ounce chopped pancetta

- In a large saucepan, melt the butter and then add the onions and sage. If the onions are not overly sweet add brown sugar. Stir occasionally as the onions caramelize – approximately 1 hour.

- Preheat oven to 400F.

- Place puff pastry sheets on a lightly floured surface. Roll out and cut each sheet into nine squares. Fold all four edges up, pinching with your fingers to create a rough rim. Score a square in the center then brush with the egg wash. Bake in the oven until golden brown, approximately 15 minutes. Place on a rack to cool and remove the center square (the scored portion should have popped up for easy removal).

- In a small frying pan, cook the pancetta until it becomes crisp.

- Place the onions in the tart shell and sprinkle a little pancetta on each tart. Tarts may be served warm or at room temperature.

chapter 1 - appetizers

gougeres by Ali Rush Carscaden, 15c Wine Shop & Bar

Gourgeres (goo/zhehr) are an amazing French cheesy puff that pairs perfectly with wine – a fun light appetite teaser that wakes up your palate for the wine to come. These savory bites are easy to make by just following the steps. Gourgerescan be made with any one of the many artisan cheeses. Bon Appetit!

- Preheat oven to 400°, line 2 baking sheets with parchment paper.

- In medium saucepan combine milk, butter, and salt and bring to a boil. Reduce temperature to low and beat in flour with a wooden spoon (a smooth dough will form). Continue to cook for about 2 minutes to cook off the flour taste. You will see a skin form around the pan.

- Transfer dough to bowl or food processor. Add eggs all at once and process until smooth. If doing without a food processor, beat in eggs one at a time. This will take a few minutes to get the dough smooth. Add gruyere and a pinch of pepper.

- Fill a pastry bag with dough and pipe out tablespoon sized mounds. Or if you don't have a pastry bag on hand, just spoon out tablespoon size mounds. Sprinkle with Parmesan cheese and bake for 16-18 minutes. They should look perfectly puffed and golden. Remove from oven to cool. If gourgeres begin to collapse, just pop back in over for 1-2 minutes.

- Serve warm or at room temperature. These little gems reheat beautifully at 350° for about 5 minutes.

Note: *You can use any cheese you like with this recipe -- just keep in mind that the wine is paired with the cheese. So for example if you use blue cheese instead of Gruyere, try pairing with a bolder, fruitier red such as a Zinfandel or Petite Sirah.*

1 cup whole milk
1 stick unsalted butter
1 teaspoon kosher salt
1 cup flour
4 farm fresh local eggs
1 cup shredded Gruyere cheese
¼ cup shredded Parmesan cheese
Pinch of ground pepper

eat this with...

Bodegas M Tempranillo
Clayhouse Malbec
Hearst Ranch Merlot
J. Lohr Merlot
Opolo Tempranillo
Pear Valley Tom's Oak Chardonnay
Ranchita Canyon Malbec
Red Soles Tempranillo
Robert Hall Merlot

rosemary shrimp skewers by Chef Joanne DeGarimore, Pier 46 Seafood

Pier 46 Seafood, located in Templeton, carries the perfect shrimp for your wallet; Large, Small and in between. Chef Joanne used Wild Mexican Shrimp, U12 which means it takes 12 or less of these beauties to make a pound. These Citrus Ginger Shrimp on Rosemary Skewers will fully satisfy four people.

Serves 4
1 thumb fresh ginger, peeled and grated
4 limes juiced, 2 zested (zest prior to juicing!)
2 lemons, zested and juiced
3 oranges, zested and juiced
3 tablespoons melted butter
3 tablespoons olive oil
1 teaspoon salt
4 rosemary skewers, leave lovely tips intact
Chopped rosemary from four rosemary skewers
1 pound wild Mexican shrimp U12, peeled, tails on

- Mix all ingredients, except shrimp and skewers, in a large bowl.

- Place shrimp in marinade. Allow to marinate from 20 minutes to an hour in refrigerator.

- Slide shrimp onto rosemary skewers. Cook over a grill or hot pan, allowing to brown slightly on the outside, making sure not to overcook.

- Serve with lime wedges.

eat this with...
Bodegas M Albariño
Calcareous Syrah
JUSTIN Rosé
LXV Rising Temp
Penman Springs Rosé
Red Soles Rosé
Robert Hall Syrah
Tablas Creek Viognier

simply incredibe pizza by Simply Incredible

This was created by a couple of Simply Incedible's loyal customers, Mika Nagamine and Jeff Cours. There are so many creative ways to incorporate smoked Alaskan wild salmon in everyday dishes!

Yield

1 10-ounce pizza crust
2 tablespoons extra virgin olive oil
½ Granny Smith apple, cored and chopped
3 ounces smoked Alaska wild salmon
¾ to 1 cup Fontina cheese, grated
1 tablespoon freshly-grated Parmesan cheese
¼ teaspoon thyme

eat this with...
Opolo Nebbiolo
Pear Valley Grenache
Robert Hall Cuvée de Robles
San Marcos Creek Nebbiolo

- Pre-heat oven to 500F

- Remove skin from salmon and cut into small cubes

- Brush pizza crust with extra virgin olive oil. Sprinkle with chopped Granny Smith apples and smoked salmon cubes. Add grated Fontina cheese to the top. Bake for 10 minutes or until cheese is golden brown. Remove from oven and, while hot, sprinkle with grated Parmesan cheese and thyme.

chapter 1 - appetizers

shrimp cocktail by Chef Natalie Dorris

This Bay Shrimp Cocktail with Mango & Pineapple recipe is a great starter for a nice dinner party or a casual backyard barbecue.

Yield

2 pounds Bay Shrimp, rinsed
4 mangos, diced
1 small pineapple, diced
1 small red onion diced
1 red bell pepper, diced
1 jalapeño, seeded and minced
2 cloves garlic, minced
2 limes, juiced
2 lemon, juiced
Salt and pepper, to taste
Corn tortilla chips

❧ Combine the shrimp and remaining ingredients, except the tortilla chips, together. Let marinate in refrigerator for 4-24 hours. Season to taste with salt and pepper. Serve in a large bowl on a bed of red cabbage with tortilla chips or spoon into individual martini glasses garnished with a chip and lime wedge.

eat this with...
Pear Valley Chardonnay
Pomar Junction Picnic Chardonnay
Robert Hall Sauvignon Blanc
Tablas Creek Grenache Blanc
Villa San Juliette

black pepper calamari by Chef Thomas Drahos, Avant-Garde Catering

The sweet and spicy sauce will have all your friends asking for the recipe when you create this gourmet calamari appetizer.

Sweet and spicy sauce
- 1 pineapple, juiced
- 1 cup brown sugar
- ½ cup rice wine vinegar
- ½ cup corn starch and water slurry
- ½ tablespoon Worcestershire sauce
- ½ knob of ginger
- 1 tablespoon sambal chili paste
- 1 Thai bird chili, diced small

Black pepper calamara
- 1 pound calamari tubes and tentacles
- 3 cups rice flour
- 3 cups bread crumbs
- 5 cups milk
- 3 tablespoons crushed black pepper

- ➛ Place all sauce ingredients, except the corn starch and water slurry, in a medium sauce pot. Bring to a boil and add the corn starch and water slurry a little at a time, just until mixture gets thick enough to coat the back of the spoon. Remove from heat and chill. Reserve until calamari is ready to serve.

- ➛ Preheat oil 350 degrees.

- ➛ Soak cleaned calamari in milk for ten minutes. Meanwhile mix flour, bread crumbs, and black pepper in a large bowl reserve. Strain milk off calamari and dredge into the flour mixture. Carefully place in hot oil, being sure that you don't overload the pot. Fry calamari until lightly golden. Remove and place on a stack of paper towels to drain oil. Repeat until all calamari is done.

- ➛ Serve with sweet and spicy sauce for dipping.

eat this with...
Bodegas M Albariño
Eberle Pinot Grigio
Pear Valley Albariño
Lone Madrone Albariño
Pear Valley Frizzante Muscat
Robert Hall Orange Muscat
Silver Horse Albariño
Still Waters Pinot Grigio
Tablas Creek Picpoul Blanc

smoked salmon mini toasts by Simply Incredible

These smoked salmon mini toast appetizers are so quick and easy you will want to make them every time you have company. Be sure to have plenty of Simply Incredible Smoked Salmon on hand.

Serves 8-10

    4 ounces Neufchatel cheese
    4 ounces goat cheese
    2 tablespoons fresh minced dill, plus 1 ounce for garnish
    1 package mini toasts (3 ounces)
    6 ounces Simply Incredible smoked salmon
    Fresh ground cracked black pepper

eat this with...

Asuncion Ridge Pinot Noir
Castoro Gewurztraminer
Clayhouse Chenin Blanc
Opolo Pinot Noir
Pear Valley Chenin Blanc
Steinbeck Viognier

- Bring the cheeses to room temperature, then blend with a hand-held mixer. Add the 2 ounces of dill until mixed thoroughly. Using a spreader knife, top each toast with the mixture.

- Break salmon into small pieces and place on top of the cheese.

- Sprinkle remaining 1 ounce of dill and ground black pepper on top to taste.

prosciutto crostini by Ranchita Canyon Vineyard

These prosciutto crostini appetizers, by Teresa Hinrichs, are one of those recipes that can be made in a very short period of time. The combination of flavors and textures will have your guests reaching for another so make plenty. This recipes also pairs with a wide range of wines, both white and red.

Yield

1 loaf baguette bread
1 package prosciutto
1 jar fig jam or apricot jam
Manchego cheese
Parsley
Olive oil

- Thinly slice baguette bread. Place on cookie sheet and lightly brown in the oven.

- Spread jam on bread. Place a piece of prosciutto on top of jam, followed by a thin slice of manchego cheese. Place a drop or two of olive oil on the cheese. Sprinkle with black pepper and garnish with a piece of parsley.

eat this with...
Christian Lazo Barbara
Ranchita Canyon Cabernet Pfeffer
Ranchita Canyon Cabernet
Robert Hall Merlot
Vista Del Rey Barbera

tandoori chicken by Neeta Mittal, LXV Wines

Unmistakable smoky flavored chicken traditionally cooked in cylindrical clay oven – a tandoor.

Serves 4-6
- **10 pieces of chicken legs and thighs**
- **2 teaspoons coarse salt**
- **Juice of one fresh lime**

Tandoori Marinade:
- **1 tablespoon melted butter**
- **1 teaspoon ground cumin**
- **1 teaspoon ground coriander**
- **1 teaspoon ground cinnamon**
- **1/2 teaspoon turmeric**
- **1 teaspoon chili powder (adjust to taste)**
- **1 cup whole milk plain yogurt**
- **2 tablespoons finely minced fresh ginger-garlic paste**
- **½ teaspoon garam masala powder**
- **Optional: few strands of saffron soaked in milk**

eat this with...
LXV Viognier Summer Satine

- Make deep cuts into the chicken. Apply lemon juice and salt to tenderize the meat. Set aside for 30 minutes.

- Hang yogurt in a muslin cloth for about 20 minutes to get rid of the whey. Mix the thick yogurt with the ingredients of the marinade and apply to the chicken. This is best done by kneading the chicken and marinade in a freezer bag. Refrigerate for at least 3 hours.

- Grill the chicken, preferably over a charcoal bbq for the "Tandoor" smokiness, basting it with butter. If you are using the oven, leave a few pieces of red hot charcoal in a steel container alongside the chicken.

darian's meatballs by Darian Buckles, Templeton Hills Beef

Templeton Hills Beef Black Angus cattle are raised from birth, grazing the lands in the community of Templeton. Even the most basic cuts of meat have more flavor and texture when raised this way. Try this meatball recipe by Darian using Templeton Hills Beef and see the difference.
This recipe can also be made in a crock pot.

Cherry BBQ Glaze
  1/2 cup cherry preserves
  1/2 cup ketchup
  1/3 cup cider vinegar
  1/4 cup olive oil
  1 tablespoon Worchestershire sauce
  1-2 cloves garlic, peeled and crushed

- Place everything in food processor or blender and blend/pulse until smooth. Refrigerate until used.

3/4 cup bread crumbs
1/4 cup milk
1 pound ground beef
1 small onion, chopped fine
1 teaspoon garlic salt
1/4 teaspoon pepper
1 tablespoon Worchestershire sauce
1 egg lightly beaten

- Soak bread crumbs in milk for 5 minutes.
- Mix together beef, onion, garlic, pepper and Worechestershire sauce. Add soaked bread crumbs and egg.
- In a frying pan heat 1-2 T olive oil to 350 degrees. Roll meat into 1 ounce balls. Fry in oil until cooked, about 5-8 minutes. This recipe freezes well and doubles or triples with no problem.
- When ready to serve, heat BBQ sauce and cover meatballs.

eat this with...
Broken Earth Merlot
Caliza Syrah
JUSTIN Cabernet Sauvignon
Pear Valley Charbono
Penman Springs Meritage
Robert Hall Merlot
Shale Oak Zinfandel
Windward Pinot Noir

chapter 1 - appetizers

lamb sliders by Robin's Restaurant

Lamb Kefta Sliders with Blue Cheese.
These little burgers deliver big flavor.

Yield

8 ounce ground lamb
8 ounce ground pork
½ minced onion
2 tablespoon vegetable oil
2 tablespoon chopped cilantro
¼ teaspoon ground cumin
¼ teaspoon ground coriander
¼ teaspoon ground cinnamon
½ teaspoon salt
A pinch of crushed dried chili
8 slider buns or rolls
4 ounces blue cheese

- Sautee onions in oil until translucent and then add dry spices and cook for 1 more minute. Add dry spices mixture, cilantro, and salt to meat and mix well.

- Make two ounce patties and gill them to medium-rare and then top it with blue cheese so that the cheese melts. It should be medium by the time the cheese melts.

- Serve them in a slider bun or roll and serve with condiments. Hummus, Tatziki, Ketchup, Mustard or pickled vegetables; make it fun!

eat this with...
Clayhouse Vineyard Malbec
Derby Cabernet Franc
Pear Valley Cabernet Franc
Red Soles Cabernet Franc
SummerWood Diosa
Tablas Creek Côtes de Tablas

chapter 2 - small plates

mushroom risotto by Il Cortile Ristorante

One of the signs of a talented Italian chef is the ability to make a good risotto.
Try this recipe from Il Cortile to impress your friends. Serve as a small plate or side.

Serves 4

1 cup Arborio rice
5 tablespoons extra virgin olive oil
½ cup of white wine
4 ½ cups of chicken stock
7 ounces mixed mushrooms
1 shallot finely chopped
2 tablespoons garlic infused oil

2 tablespoons brandy
1 tablespoons thyme
¼ cup heavy cream
Salt and pepper
3 tablespoons Parmesean cheese
Touch of truffle oil

eat this with...

Anglim Pinot Noir
Cass Grenache
J. Lohr Highlands Bench Pinot Noir
Halter Ranch Grenache
Pear Valley Pinot Noir
Pretty-Smith Palette de Rouge
Robert Hall Cuvee de Robles
Tablas Creek Côtes de Tablas
Windward Pinot Noir

- Bring the chicken stock to a steady simmer in a saucepan.

- Heat 3 tablespoons olive oil in a heavy 4-quart pan over moderate heat. Add the rice and stir with a wooden spoon to make sure all the grains are well coated.

- Add the white wine and stir until the wine is completely absorbed. Add 1 cup of the simmering stock, stirring frequently. Set the risotto to the side .

- Heat 2 tablespoons olive oil in another pan. Add the chopped shallots and stir until shallots are soft. Add the garlic infused oil. Stir for another minute. Add the mushrooms, salt and pepper and thyme and continue stirring. Add to the rice and stir. Add the stock ½ c at a time and stir until the liquid is absorbed each time. Continue until the rice is to the desired consistency, preferably al dente. Add the brandy and stir. Add the cream and stir. Once everything is combined well and ready to plate, add the truffle oil and stir one last time.

- Plate the risotto into pasta bowls and serve.

beets with blackberry basil sauce by Pat Lareau

Your guests will be surprised by the combination of flavors in this dish. The presentation with contrasting colors is spectacular.

Serves 4

4 medium raw red beets in their skins
2 cups ripe blackberries
Sprig fresh culinary lavender
3 tablespoons salted butter
1 tablespoon light soy sauce
1 tablespoon balsamic vinegar
Leaves from 4 sprigs of basil, coarsely chopped
1 cup milk (optional)

Cook the beets in salted water for 30-60 minutes depending on size. Allow to cool in the water. When cool enough to handle, but still warm, peel. Cut each in quarters from the top to the stem end and set aside reassembled as a ball, assuring the bottom is flat enough to stand for presentation. Meanwhile melt the butter in a sauté pan over low heat. Add the blackberries and crush them with a fork as they heat up. Cook until the mixture is juicy, about 5 more minutes. Add the soy, vinegar and basil leaves and leave over very low heat without stirring for 4-5 minutes.

Emulsify the milk by putting it in a cappuccino frother. Only the foam is used to garnish this dish. This can be omitted if you do not have a cappuccino frother. The flavors of the dish are not impacted.

Put some berries on each plate. Position one whole beet standing up on each plate. Drizzle sauce over the beets and put the rest over the berries. If using the emulsified milk, put a dollop on top before sprinkling with lavender flowers. If you are lucky enough to have French Lavender in your garden, a spring makes a lovely accompaniment.

eat this with...

Ancient Peaks Rosé
Cass Sparkling
Clavo Sparkling
Clayhouse Pink
Derby Sparkling
Graveyard Pink
J. Lohr Riesling
Le Vigne Sparkling
Pear Valley Rosé

eggplant crisp by Chef Jacob Lovejoy, Cass Café

Japanese eggplant crisp, tomato confit, buffalo bocconcini.

Serves 6-8

1 package buffalo Bocconcini (small, fresh buffalo mozzarella)
1 quart frying oil, such as peanut
½ cup all-purpose flour
Kosher salt and fresh ground pepper
2 large eggs, lightly beaten
1 cup Panko, Japanese bread crumbs
2 medium Japanese eggplants, cut crosswise into ¼ inch thick slices
1 batch tomato confit (see recipe on right hand side)
5 fresh basil leaves, chiffonade

- Preheat the oven to 375F degrees.

- Heat the frying oil in a small, deep saucepan over medium high heat (or until a frying thermometer reads 360 degrees). Place the flour, seasoned with salt and pepper, the beaten eggs, and the panko in separate side by side by side shallow bowls. Dredge the eggplant in the flour, then dip in the egg, then finally coat with breadcrumbs. Fry the eggplant in batches until golden brown. Transfer to a paper towel to drain.

- Cut the mozzarella balls in half. Arrange slices on a baking sheet, top with a slice of the tomato confit, then one half of a mozzarella ball. Bake for just a few minutes until the cheese starts to melt, and remove.

- Place onto a platter and top with the fresh basil.

Tomatoes confit:

3 tablespoons extra virgin olive oil
Salt
Freshly ground white pepper
3 cloves garlic, finely sliced
10 basil leaves, torn
4 sprigs thyme, leaves only
2 bay leaves, broken
20 ripe plum tomatoes, peeled
1/4 to 1/2 teaspoon sugar

❧ Center a rack in the oven and preheat the oven to 200F. Line a baking sheet with foil and pour about 2 tablespoons olive oil evenly over the pan. Sprinkle the oil with salt and pepper. Strew a little of the garlic, basil, thyme, and bay leaves over the oil. Cut each tomato lengthwise in half and carefully, with your fingers or a tiny spoon, remove the seeds. Lay the tomato halves cut side down in the pan, wiggling the tomatoes around if necessary so that each tomato has a gloss of oil on its cut side. Using a pastry brush, give the tops of the tomatoes a light coat of olive oil. Season the tops of the tomatoes with salt and pepper and a little sugar, and scatter over the rest of the garlic, basil, thyme, and bay leaves. Slide the pan into the oven and bake the tomatoes for 2 1/2 hours, or until they are very tender but still able to hold their shape; turn the tomatoes over at half-time and open the oven for just a second every 30 minutes or so to get rid of the moisture that will build up in the oven. Cool the tomatoes to room temperature on their pan.

eat this with...

Cass Rosé

goat cheese parcels by Pat Lareau, travel-and-eat.blogspot.com

Serves 6

For goat cheese parcels

2 tablespoons unsalted butter, melted
8 ounces soft mild goat cheese , at room temperature
3 tablespoons heavy cream
1 large egg
1/2 teaspoon Dijon mustard
1/4 teaspoon black pepper
3 (17- by 12-inch) sheets phyllo dough, thawed if frozen

For compote

3 cups French fine green beans, cut in thirds crosswise
1/4 cup Sun dried tomatoes in oil - chopped
2 Scallions - sliced thin, including some greens
4 Basil leaves, chopped
Zest of 1 lemon
1/4 cup dressing made from balsamic vinegar, salt, pepper, culinary lavender, olive oil

- Put oven rack in middle position and preheat oven to 375°F. Brush muffin tins with some melted butter.

- Stir together goat cheese, cream, egg, mustard, and pepper in a bowl until combined well.

- Keep phyllo sheets covered with 2 overlapping sheets of plastic wrap and then a dampened kitchen towel to prevent drying. Arrange 1 sheet of phyllo on a work surface, then brush with some melted butter. Cut phyllo into 4 (8 1/2- by 6-inch) rectangles and arrange 2 of them one over the other in a crisscross pattern, then line a muffin cup with overlapping phyllo. Repeat procedure lining remaining 5 muffin cups.

- Spoon goat cheese filling into cups and loosely gather edges of phyllo over center (if pieces of phyllo break off, arrange in center). Bake phyllo parcels until tops are golden brown and sides are golden, 25 to 35 minutes, then transfer from pan to a rack to cool slightly.

- Make the compote: Steam beans crisp-tender. Drain and rinse in cold water. Combine softened dried tomatoes with the beans. Add the scallion and basil. Cover and refrigerate until ready to serve.

- Make the dressing: Combine and allow to stand at room temperature until ready to use.

- At serving time, lightly dress bean mixture with balsamic vinaigrette (dressing sooner could turn the beans yellow), add additional basil and lemon zest. Place some compote on each plate, sprinkle with pancetta, and place a cheese parcel on top of it.

steak tartare by Chef Laurent Grangien, Bistro Laurent

This classic French dish turns an every day lunch into something special.
Select a high quality lean cut of beef for this dish.

Serves 6

1 ½ pounds beef (filet or top sirloin)
2 egg yolks
2 shallots
2 tablespoons Dijon mustard
Cornichons chopped (or capers)
Finely cut chives
2 lemons juiced
Salt and pepper, to taste
1/4 teaspoon cayenne pepper
Olive Oil

- Hand cut the beef into a very small dice.

- Add salt, pepper and cayenne pepper, followed by shallots, mustard, cornichons, lemon juice, drop of olive oil, then egg yolks. Mix everything with a spoon.

- Serve with green salad or pomme frites.

eat this with...

Clavo Collusion
Clavo Sparkling
DAOU Syrah
Derby Sparkling
Eberle Syrah
J. Lohr Pinot Noir
Windward Pinot Noir

spicy shrimp romesco by Chef Andre Averseng, Paso Terra Seafood

These shrimp with the spicy romesco sauce are perfect served over roasted spaghetti squash.

Serves 8

2 large tomatoes, broiled
1 roasted bell pepper
2 oounces olive oil
3 cloves garlic minced
Bread crumbs and 2 oz almond meal
Paprika and red pepper flakes
10 ounces red wine vinegar
Salt & pepper, to taste
2 pound spaghetti squash
2 ounces butter
1 pound shrimp (16 – 20 count)

- For the sauce: Peel tomatoes, remove seeds from pepper and cut coarsely. Sauté in Olive Oil with garlic. Add bread crumbs and almond meal. Add paprika and pepper flakes, vinegar and cook down. Adjust seasoning with salt and pepper. Process in food processor.

- Marinate shrimp in Cajun style spice with olive oil for ½ hour. Do not add salt.

- Bake spaghetti squash in 375 degree oven for 40 minutes until soft. Cut open and scrape inside with fork to remove all the flesh. Sauté in butter with salt and pepper.

- Sauté shrimp in oil, add salt and cook very fast in hot pan.

- Portion squash on serving plates, add shrimp and pour romesco sauce over top. Garnish with parsley or micro herbs.

eat this with...
Bodegas M Tempranillo
Graveyard Tempranillo
J. Lohr Tempranillo
JUSTIN Sauvignon Blanc
Niner Sauvignon Blanc
Pear Valley Tempranillo
Red Soles Tempranillo
Summerwood Viognier

mahi mahi lettuce wraps by Lisa Pretty

These lettuce wraps are perfect for backyard parties. Feel free to substitute your favorite fish in this recipe.

Serves 4

1 pound Mahi Mahi, cut into 1-2 inch strips
1 teaspoon olive oil
Juice from ½ fresh lemon
1 teaspoon cayenne pepper
1 tablespoon dried thyme
Salt and pepper to taste

Sauce

1 cup non fat Greek yogurt
½ cup fresh cilantro, chopped
3 cloves garlic, finely chopped
Juice from ½ fresh lemon

½ cup red cabbage, chopped
½ cup green cabbage, chopped
1 avocado, sliced
3 green onions, chopped
12 cherry tomatoes, quartered
5 radishes, sliced
2 jalapeno peppers, sliced
1 head of bib, butter or iceberg lettuce, separated into leaves

- Wash the fish and pat dry. Rub with oil, lemon juice, cayenne, thyme, salt and pepper. Place in refrigerator until ready to grill.

- Mix together all sauce ingredients. Place chopped cabbage in a bowl and toss with sauce. This can be done a couple of hours prior to serving.

- Place fish in a grilling basket and grill for 1-2 minutes per side over medium heat. Take care not to over cook or fish will be dry.

- Place all ingredients on a large platter or individual bowls. Have your guest take a lettuce leaf and load it up with all their favorite ingredients.

eat this with...
Castoro Cellars Pinot Blanc
Eos Pinot Blanc
Halter Ranch Cotes de Paso Blanc
Robert Hall Grenache Blanc
Steinbeck Viognier
Vina Robles White[4]

niçoise salad sandwich by Chef Laurent Grangien, Bistro Laurent

It is a classic salad Niçoise served on toasted bread!

Serves 6

6 slices of "Pain de campagne"
6 tablespoons olive tapenade
Olives niçoises
3 hard boiled eggs
1 pound "haricots verts"
1 pound potatoes
1 red bell pepper
1 white onion
1 pound ahi tuna
12 filets anchovies in oil
Salt and pepper, to taste

- Spread tapenade on the toast.
- Arrange tomatoes, eggs, potatoes, and haricots verts on toast. Alternate the 4 ingredients when arranging.
- Next, place the ahi then the anchovies on top of the vegetables.
- Finally place the olives, sliced onions and bell peppers
- Sprinkle with salt and pepper.

eat this with...
Bodegas M Albariño
Clavo Enigma
Pear Valley Albariño
Robert Hall Cuvée de Robles
Shale Oaks Rosé
Silver Horse Albariño
Tablas Creek Côtes de Tablas

chapter 2 - small plates

mano de leon scallop by Chef Jacob, Cass Café

Mano de Leon scallops with Meyer lemon and chili pistou, topped with spicy microgreens. Delicious.

Serves 6

6 fresh Mano de Leon scallops, adductor muscle removed
2 tablespoon unsalted butter
Kosher salt and fresh cracked pepper
Juice and zest from 2 Meyer lemons
2 cloves garlic
1 jalapeno, seeds and pith removed
¼ cup olive oil
½ cup curly parsley leaves
1 container spicy microgreens

- Rinse the scallops and pat dry with a clean paper towel. Season with salt and pepper.

- In a medium skillet over medium high heat, melt the butter. Add the scallops and sear until golden brown on each side, approximately 3 minutes per side. Remove from pan and set aside.

- For the pistou: In a food processor or blender, combine juice and zest, garlic, jalapeno, and parsley. Pulse a few times, then slowly drizzle in the olive oil. Pulse a few more times, season with salt and pepper to taste, and chill.

- Place a single scallop on a small plate, top with a small spoonful of the pistou, and garnish with the microgreens.

eat this with...
Cass Viognier

prawn and scallop pie by Chef Charles D. Paladin Wayne

The crust can be filled with almost anything. Chef Charlie choose prawn and scallops with a lobster sauce for his "meat pies".

Serves 6-8

Short Crust
2/3 cup shortening, butter, or Lard
1 tablespoon white vinegar
1/3 cup ice cold water
2 cups all- purpose flour
½ teaspoon salt

- Using a mixer, or a food processor, combine flour salt and shortening. This will begin to look like crumbs. Add slowly the iced water and the Vinegar. Depending on the age of the flour you might need a very small amount of water; the dough should be supple but holds together. Knead for 2-3 minutes, then wrap in cellophane and refrigerate for 1 hour to overnight. Take out when you are ready to use.

- Preheat an oven to 350 degrees. Knead the dough (if crumbly, tear into small pieces and sprinkle with water and re knead the dough. Place on a lightly floured board and sprinkle with flour. Roll out to 1/8th inch thick. Using a round cookie cutter cut 3 inch circles and form into a large greased muffin pan. Cut squares of parchment and line the pastry and use beans or baking beads to weight the dough to keep shape. Bake at 350 until lightly browned.

- Remove and cool. Remove parchment and weights. Store shells in an airtight container, for up to two weeks, in a cool place.

Prawns and Scallops in Lobster Sauce

12-15 large shrimp, peeled and deveined
12- large fresh sea scallops
1 tablespoon olive oil
2 tablespoons unsalted butter
1/4 cup sherry
3 tablespoons all- purpose flour
1 tablespoons lobster paste
2 cups heavy cream
½ cup fresh English peas
½ cup fresh diced shallot
1/2 cup brunoised carrot
Fresh Ground Pepper and Sea Salt
Micro Greens (for garnish)
Truffle or olive oil (to dress greens for finish)

***CHEF'S PROFILE:** Chef Charles D. Paladin Wayne*

Chef Charlie has been in the business of cooking for 38+ years, starting in the southwest, traveling around the world, and for the last 26 years, making his home on the central coast. The allure of the ever growing wine industry, and the availability of fresh local products, has made him a permanent resident.

His business "Catering by Chef Charlie" was started in the summer of '95 and has grown in popularity as one of the best "Quality" choices for weddings, wine dinners, everything food & service related.

- Heat a large skillet over medium high heat.

- Toss the shrimp and scallops in the olive oil and salt and pepper. Sear the shrimp and scallop for two minutes on each side then set aside.

- Sauté the shallots in the same pan, add butter, then sherry, then flour. Stir into a roux, add cream and bring to a slow boil. Add the carrots and the fresh English peas.

- When ready to serve add the Shrimp and Scallop for three to four minutes. Fill the Pastry Shell on the serving plate allowing the sauce to run over a bit. Add 2 Shrimp and two scallops stacked in the shell top with Micro Greens tossed in a light amount of oil (truffle or olive oil) and serve.

eat this with...
Caliza Sidekick
Broken Earth Reserve Petit Verdot
Pomar Junction Viognier
Tablas Creek Patelin de Tablas Blanc

crab cakes by Chef Ryan Swarthout

Crab Cakes with Papaya Slaw and Sweet Thai Chili Sauce

Crab Cake
- **1 pound crab meat**
- **2 tablespoon ginger, minced**
- **2/3 cup red onion, minced**
- **1 lemon, zest and juice**
- **1 lime, zest and juice**
- **¼ cup soy sauce**
- **1 tablespoon Sriracha sauce**
- **½ cup mayonnaise**
- **½ cup panko bread crumbs**
- **2 cups panko bread crumbs, reserve for coating**

Papaya Slaw
- **½ cup papaya, small diced**
- **¼ cup red bell, small diced**
- **2 each green onions, sliced**
- **¼ cup mayonnaise**
- **2 tablespoons sesame oil**
- **2 tablespoons rice vinegar**
- **2 tablespoons sugar**

- For Crab Cakes: Place all ingredients except extra panko in a large bowl and mix together. Form into patties and coat with extra panko. Heat 2 tablespoons of olive oil in a large pan over medium heat. Working in batches, sauté on each for 2 minutes or until brown and heated through.

- For Papaya Slaw: Mix the mayonnaise, sesame oil, rice vinegar and sugar together and set aside. Place the diced papaya, red bell peppers and green onions in a separated bowl and drizzle enough dressing to coat. Season if needed.

- Garnish your crab cakes with the papaya slaw and sweet thai chili sauce.

eat this with...
Cass Sparkling
Clavo Sparkling
Le Vigne Sparkling
Pear Valley Our Daily White
Penman Springs Rosé
Shale Oaks Rosé
Tablas Creek Picpoul Blanc

guilt-free BLT by Simply Incredible

These Bacon, Lettuce and Tomato sandwiches are guilt-free since they are made with Alaskan Salmon Bacon and homemade mayonnaise. Kylee's Alaskan Salmon Bacon can be ordered from simplyincredible.com.

Serves 4

8-12 slices of Kylee's Alaskan Salmon Bacon
8 slices of white or whole wheat bread
8 leaves of romaine or iceberg lettuce
8 slices of ripened tomatoes
8 tablespoons of mayonnaise (see recipe on right)

- Cook bacon according to directions (lightly oiled pan, medium-high heat, 1 minute each side). Meanwhile, toast the bread slices. Spread 1 tablespoon mayonnaise on each slice of toasted bread.

- Add 1-2 slices of lettuce to the mayo toast slice. Add 2-3 slices of tomato on top of lettuce. Arrange 3 slices of bacon evenly on top of the tomato. Add 1-2 slices of lettuce on top of bacon. Put the remaining mayo-spread toast slice on top to finish the sandwich.

Easy Homemade Mayonnaise

1 whole pastured egg (at room temperature)
1 pastured egg yolk (at room temperature)
1 teaspoon organic Dijon-style mustard
1 ½ tablespoon lemon juice (freshly squeezed)
½ cup extra virgin olive oil
½ cup extra virgin coconut oil (melted/cooled slightly)
Pinch or two of sea salt or kosher salt

- In a blender, add egg, egg yolk, mustard, lemon juice and salt. Process about 30 seconds. Combine oils in a small container or measuring cup. With the blender running at medium-high, add the oil slowly to egg mixture in a very thin stream (about the thickness of a pencil lead) through the blender top. Taste and adjust seasonings (add more salt or lemon juice). Place in a glass jar with a tight-fitting lid. It will firm up in the refrigerator, and it will last about two weeks.

eat this with...

Alta Colina Grenache
Hug Cellars Grenache
Pear Valley Inspiration
Robert Hall Merlot
Summerwood Merlot

fish with fennel by Tablas Creek Vineyard

This simple Mediterranean fish preparation pairs well with Grenache Blanc or Roussanne, or blends of those. The fish with fennel makes a wonderful first course or serve in large portions as a main dish.

Serves 4-6

1 pound meaty, flaky white fish (like cod)
1 bulb fennel, sliced
1 shallot, sliced
4 cloves garlic, roughly chopped
4 small plum tomatoes, peeled and diced
2 tablespoons olive oil
1 1/2 cups dry white wine
Juice of 1/2 lemon
1 large sprig parsley, chopped
Fresh-ground black pepper, to taste
Salt, to taste

- Heat olive oil over medium heat in a large saucepan. Add the fennel and shallots and saute for a few minutes until they start to soften. Add garlic and saute for 2 minutes.

- Add wine and turn heat up to medium-high. Boil for 3 minutes. Add tomatoes and boil for 2 minutes.

- Submerge fillets in bottom of saucepan; add salt and pepper to taste. Cover, reduce heat to low and cook until fish flakes easily -- about 10 minutes.

- Add lemon juice, and adjust seasonings. Ladle into bowls, top with parsley, and serve with crusty bread for dipping.

eat this with...
Tablas Creek Grenache Blanc
Tablas Creek Esprit de Beaucastel Blanc
Tablas Creek Roussanne
Tablas Creek Côtes de Tablas Blanc

pan seared black cod by Chef Thomas Drahos, Avant-Garde Catering

Seared black cod, smoked grapes and Cognac flambéed bay scallops offer a wonderful combination of flavors.

Cod

1 ounce olive oil
½ teaspoon salt
½ teaspoon black pepper
6 black cod fillets

- Preheat oven to 350 degrees. Heat medium sauté pan over medium heat and add oil once smoke appears from the pan. Place cod presentation side down and sear until golden crust forms flip and place in the oven for 8 minutes or until firm and done.

Smoked Grapes

1 pound of red grapes
4 cups of onion husk (soaked in water)
½ teaspoon salt
½ teaspoon black pepper

- In the bottom layer of a steamer pot place the soaked onion husk and heat the pot over very low heat. Add the grapes in the top layer and cover. Let smoke for 15 minutes or until done (they should just be plump not soggy).

eat this with...
Bodegas Paso Robles Albariño
Pear Valley Albariño
Robert Hall Chardonnay

Salsify bur blanc

- **3 each salsify roots(peeled ,boiled and then pureed)**
- **½ pound of (butter cut into cubes)**
- **1 shallot cut into rings**
- **1 bunch thyme**
- **1 bay leaf**
- **2 each peppercorns**
- **2 cups white wine**

- ❧ Put everything except the salsify and butter into a sauce pot and reduce until the pan is almost dry. Remove from heat and incorporate the butter one cube at a time using a whisk and making sure each cube is melted before you add more. Strain and reserve for fish.

Cognac flambéed bay scallops

- **1 pound bay scallops**
- **1 ounce of oil**
- **1 ounce cognac**
- **1 tablespoon shallots diced small**
- **1 tablespoon butter**
- **1 tablespoon cream**
- **Salt and pepper, to taste**

- ❧ Preheat a medium sauté pan over high heat. Add the oil followed by the scallops, then the shallots. cook for about two minutes. Remove from heat add the cognac and place back over the fire cook until the flame stops. Add the butter and cream. Taste and adjust seasoning using salt and pepper.

- ❧ To plate, place a few spoonfuls of the salsify bur blanc on a large plate in the middle. Next carefully place the scallops in the center of the bur blanc and then the cod on top of the scallops. Finally place the a pile of smoked grapes right on top of the fish.

CHEF'S PROFILE: Chef Thomas Drahos

Thomas grew up just outside of Bradley, CA on a fifty five acre ranch where he learned how to properly turn soil, sow seeds, and harvest fruit. He also spent his youth learning how to butcher. The two experiences at a young age led to the almost pre-destined decision to become a chef.

Thomas enrolled in the culinary arts program at Johnson & Wales University in Denver, CO. Upon graduation, Thomas moved back to California to work for Windows on the Water in Morro Bay as the Pastry Chef. He was then offered the role as Executive Chef at Fenomenal restaurant in Paso Robles, his home town.

Chef Thomas, along with a couple of friends, launched Avant-garde Catering. He came up with the idea of the traveling pop up restaurant. The idea is not new by any means but coupled with Chef Drahos talents and ability to wow guest with every turn, it would be truly an Avant-grade experience!

jambalaya pasta by Ian McPhee, McPhee's Grill

McPhee's jambalaya pasta is a hearty enough dish that it could be served as a main course. Ian likes to use Orecchiette (little ears) pasta when he makes this recipe -- you can pick your favorite.

Serves 4-6

2 tablespoons olive oil
2 ounces Andouille sausage, diced
4 ounces boneless chicken breast, sliced
6 medium shrimp, peeled
2 tablespoons chopped green onions
2 tablespoons chopped red bell pepper
2 cloves garlic, minced
1 tablespoon Chef Paul's Cajun seafood magic seasoning
2 ounces chicken stock
¼ cup Sadie Kendall's Crème Fraiche
½ teaspoon Worcestershire sauce
3-4 dashes Tabasco sauce
4 ounces favorite pasta
Chives and parmesan cheese, for garnish

eat this with...
Halter Ranch Sauvignon Blanc
Pear Valley Cabernet Franc
Ranchita Canyon Zinfandel
Robert Hall Chardonnay
Robert Hall Pape de Robles
Shale Oak Zinfandel

- In fry pan add olive oil, Andouille sausage, garlic, peppers, onions & chicken. Cook until chicken is ½ done.

- Add Seafood Magic, Tabasco and Worcestershire sauce cook for 1 minute. Add chicken stock cook 1 minute, add crème fraiche & shrimp cook until shrimp is done. Add pasta and cook to coat pasta.

- Serve in a bowl topped with a little parmesan & chives

asian quail by Lisa Pretty

Grilled quail is one of my favorite appetizers. Traditionally this is the first meal I make on a camping trip. Although there are many marinades that work, for some reason I tend to like Asian flavors on the bird.

Serves 4

4 quail, split open

Marinade

1/4 cup rice vinegar
1/4 cup soy sauce
1/4 cup sesame oil
2 cloves garlic, finely chopped
1 tablespoon ginger, finely chopped
1 teaspoon dried chili peppers

- Place quail zip lock bag. Mix together marinade ingredients and pour over quail, shake to coat, seal bag, removing as much air as possible, and place in refrigerator. Marinate for 1 hour then remove quail from bag and discard marinade.

- Grill quail over medium heat for approximately 3-4 minutes per side. Serve on a bed of sautéed Asian vegetables or fresh greens.

eat this with...

Eos Pinot Blanc
Opolo Pinot Grigio
Pear Valley Our Daily White
Red Soles Viognier
Robert Hall Grenache Blanc
Shale Oak Albariño
Still Waters Pinot Gris
Tablas Creek Vermentino

lamb tacos by Lisa Pretty

When it comes to lamb, there are certain flavor combinations that I really enjoy. Rosemary and garlic are my "go to" herbs while cucumber and yogurt are wonderful accents. I decided to skip the traditional taco toppings and instead focus on what went well with the lamb. I did keep cilantro and jalapeños as optional traditional toppings to boost the flavor while letting guests decide on the amount of each they desired.

Serves 4

1 tablespoon finely chopped fresh rosemary
1 tablespoon chopped fresh thyme
1 tablespoon olive oil
1 teaspoon ground black pepper
1.5 pounds of lamb shoulder steaks
½ cup non-fat Greek yogurt
4 cloves of garlic, finely chopped

1 English cucumber, peeled and coarsely chopped
¼ cup salad greens, torn
8 small tortillas (your choice of corn or flour)
2 jalapeño peppers, sliced
¼ cup chopped fresh cilantro
Salt to taste

- Mix together rosemary, thyme, olive oil and pepper. Rub mixture over lamb steaks then place in zip lock bag and allow to marinate for 2-6 hours in refrigerator.

- Combine yogurt, garlic and cucumber in a medium bowl. This can be done up to 1 day in advance if stored in refrigerator.

- Bring lamb to room temperature then season with salt. Grill lamb steaks for 3 minutes per side over medium heat. Remove lamb from grill and allow to rest for 5 minutes prior to slicing into bite sized pieces.

- While the lamb is resting, heat tortillas on the grill for just 15-30 seconds per side. Place salad greens over tortillas, layer with the cucumber-yogurt mixture and top with lamb. Serve with cilantro and jalapenos, on the side, as optional toppings.

eat this with...
Adelaida Cellars Cabernet Franc
Alta Colina Grenache
Caliza Grenache
Cass Mourvédre
Kenneth Volk Cabernet Franc
Opolo Cabernet Franc
Pear Valley Cabernet Franc
Ranchita Canyon Malbec
Robert Hall Pape de Robles

chapter 3 - salads

butter leaf salad by Will Torres, The Restaurant at JUSTIN

Beechers Cheddar, Apple, Radish, Fine Herbs, Buttermilk Vinaigrette

Serves 4
- 1 radish, sliced thin
- 1 Gravenstein Apple, cored, cut in 1/8ths
- 4 ounces Beechers White Cheddar, shaved thin
- 2-3 tablespoons fresh fine herbs (chive, chervil, Tarragon, Parsley), chopped fine

Buttermilk Vinaigrette:
- 1 small shallot bulb, diced fine
- ¼ cup champagne vinegar
- 1 cup buttermilk (or plain Greek yogurt)
- ¼ cup extra-virgin olive oil
- 2 tablespoons sugar
- 1 two-finger pinch Maldon flake salt
- 5-6 grinds black pepper
- 2 small heads butter leaf, broken into leaves, washed and dried
- Maldon flake salt for the table

- To make the vinaigrette, combine the diced shallot and vinegar in a small cup. Set aside for at least 15 minutes. The longer the shallots soak in the vinegar, the more their natural sugars will dissolve in the liquid and the sweeter the vinaigrette will be. Then add in buttermilk, sugar, salt and pepper. Slowly drizzle in the olive oil, whisking constantly to make sure it stays emulsified. Check seasoning.

- As soon as the dressing is ready, put the lettuce leaves in a salad bowl. Add the dressing and toss to coat with wooden salad utensils or your hands. You are less likely to bruise the lettuce if you toss it with your hands. Serve on individual salad plates or bowls; season each salad with an additional pinch of Maldon salt. Garnish salads with apple, radish, Beecher's cheddar and the fine herbs.

> **eat this with...**
> JUSTIN Sauvignon Blanc

tomato salad by Robin's Restaurant

HEIRLOOM TOMATO & FRESH MOZZARELLA SALAD WITH WALNUT VINAIGRETTE DRESSING

Serves 6-8

    3 pounds of heirloom tomatoes
    Basil salt
    Bunch of maché greens or purslane
    ½ pound of fresh mozzarella

Toasted walnut vinaigrette

    4 cup white wine
    1/2 cup white wine vinegar
    2 tablespoons garlic, minced
    2 shallots, minced
    2 teaspoon sugar
    3 ounces lemon juice
    2 1/2 cups pomace olive oil
    2 cups walnuts, toasted & finely chopped
    ½ cup chives, chopped

- For vinaigrette: In a saucepan reduce white wine by half (approximately 5-7 minutes). Set aside to cool. In separate bowl, combine white wine vinegar, garlic, shallots, sugar, & lemon juice. Add in cooled white wine reduction. Slowly whisk in the pomace olive oil to emulsify. Add in walnuts & chives.

- Slice tomatoes 5/8 thick and arrange on serving dish. Sprinkle with touch of basil salt. Shred cheese and scatter on top of tomatoes. Top with greens. Spoon dressing over and serve.

eat this with...
    Clayhouse Adobe White
    Vina Robles White [4]

greek salad by Julie Simon, Thomas Hill Organics

This salad is classic and very low maintenance. But! Even in California there is a tomato season and you should wait for it. The secret to a good greek salad is seasonal, fresh ingredients.

Serves 4

1 pound of heirloom tomatoes, any color and shape
1 English cucumber, sliced
1/2 sweet red onion, thinly sliced
A handful of Kalamata olives, pitted
1 red bell pepper
1/4 cup feta cheese
A few sprigs of each: fresh thyme, basil, mint
1 to 2 lemons, zest and juice
A generous drizzle of extra virgin olive oil
Sea salt and cracked pepper

- Cut the tomatoes into small wedges
- Place all ingredients into a bowl and toss
- Let the salad to rest for 30 minutes to allow the flavors to marry

Chef Julie recommends saving the salad bowl to reuse the beautiful juices. Let's face it, that is the best part and it is also your next salad dressing.

eat this with...
Broken Earth Pinot Gris
Castoro Pinot Grigio
Chronic Cellars Riesling
Halter Ranch Rosé
J. Lohr Riesling
Le Vigne Pinto Grigio
Red Soles Loose Laces Rosé
Shale Oak Rosé

Caesar Salad by Kevin Hyland, Paso Robles Inn Steakhouse

Chef Kevin puts a fun twist on the classic caesar by grilling the lettuce. Be sure to use a BBQ or open flame charbroiler. This is a guest favorite at the Paso Robles Inn Steakhouse -- try it at home.

Serves 2

- 1 head romaine lettuce, outer leaves trimmed
- ½ cup roasted, salted pepitas
- ½ cup grated parmesan cheese
- ¾ cup garlic sourdough crotons
- 3 tablespoon Balsamic reduction glaze
- 2 tablespoon olive oil
- ¼ teaspoon salt
- ¼ teaspoon ground black pepper

Dressing:

- 2 egg yolks
- 1 cup olive oil
- 1/3 cup red wine vinegar
- 1 tablespoon Dijon mustard
- ½ cup grated parmesan cheese
- 1 teaspoon anchovy paste
- 1/4 teaspoon ground black pepper
- 1/4 teaspoon kosher salt
- ¼ teaspoon Worcestershire sauce
- Juice of ½ lemon

- Dressing preparation: In a mixer, place egg yolks, whip 2 minutes. Add anchovy paste, Dijon, parmesan cheese, mix 2 minutes. Add oil in slowly while mixer is on medium speed, after all oil is incorporated, add lemon and red wine vinegar slowly, then add salt, pepper Worcestershire sauce. Set in refrigerator to chill.

- Preheat BBQ or charbroiler to medium

- Cut head of romaine in half, brush both sides with olive oil. Sprinkle both sides with salt and pepper. Grill 1 minute each side. Set romaine on a cutting board and cut the core out of the lettuce. Cut each section in half.

- On a round dinner size plate crisscross two half of the salad. Drizzle with dressing, add croutons, pepitas, parmesan cheese, then drizzle with balsamic reduction

eat this with...

Aron Hill Primitivo
Cypher Tempranillo
Bella Luna Sangiovese
Eberle Sangiovese
Halter Ranch Sauvignon Blanc
LXV Rising Tempo
Opolo Sangiovese
Tobin James Zinfandel
Zenaida Cellars Primitivo

salad lyonnaise by Chef Kelly Wangard, SummerWood Inn

This sophisticated salad by Chef Kelly is perfect for the warm days of summer. She recommends serving this with toasted bread for a satisfying light meal.

Serves 2
- 2 eggs
- 1 handful of spinach, sliced thin
- 1 handful of frisée lettuce
- 1 ear fresh corn, cut off and cooked, then cooled
- 2 strips bacon, cooked then sliced thin
- ¼ red onion, sliced thin

Vinaigrette
- 1 tablespoon red wine vinegar
- 1 teaspoon Dijon mustard
- 3 tablespoons olive oil
- ½ teaspoon oregano
- Pinch salt and pepper

- Combine all vinaigrette ingredients, shake in a jar or whisk together in a bowl.

- Heat a pot of water to boiling.

- Toss together spinach, lettuce, corn, red onion, and bacon with a small amount of the dressing. Divide between two plates.

- Crack the eggs into boiling water. Allow to cook for 3-4 minutes or until the whites of the eggs are white and not translucent. Carefully take out of the boiling water with a slotted spoon and carefully place atop of the dressed salad.

- Grate fresh parmesan over the top and cracked black pepper.

eat this with...
Caliza Viognier
Derby Sparkling
JUSTIN Rosé
SummerWood Diosa Blanc
SummerWood Viognier
Tablas Creek Rosé

super salad by Michele Knecht, Seasonal Custom Cuisine Delivered

When it comes to healthful and tasty foods Michele Knecht is an excellent source for great recipes. Michele's business, Seasonal Custom Cuisine Delivered, is a gourmet personal chef service with delivery throughout San Louis Obispo County. According to Michele "My husband, a white flour, white sugar, red meat luvin' cwboy, will wrinkle his nose and turn down anything offered with the word "kale" or "quinoa" attached. However, if I just put this one down in front of him he will eat and enjoy it. The kale is milder in flavor if I steam it like this rather than sauté or braise it. And at just 197calories per cup, it doesn't hurt to add a little sprinkle of feta if you like."

Six 1-cup servings

1 cup red quinoa
2 cup vegetable broth
1 cup cooked brown rice
2 cups thinly sliced fresh kale
1 cups julienne or shredded carrot
2 tablespoons toasted pine nuts
1/8 cup thinly sliced mint leaves
½ cup lemon juice - Meyer lemon is delicious
2 tablespoons olive oil
Sea salt & pepper to taste

This salad can be stored in the refrigerator for up to one week. Leftovers are perfect for a quick lunch or even breakfast.

- Toast quinoa in dry pan till fragrant (approximately 3 minutes). Add vegetable broth, top with carrots and kale. Bring to boil, reduce heat cover and simmer for 15 minutes. Fluff with a fork and add cooked brown rice, mint and pine nuts.

- Whisk lemon juice, olive oil, salt & pepper, adjust to taste. Toss dressing with salad.

eat this with...

Anglim Syrah
Eberly Syrah
Halter Ranch Zinfandel
Pear Valley Grenache
Penman Springs Rosé
Robert Hall Zinfandel
Shale Oak Syrah
Tablas Creek Rosé
Tobin James Merlot

tabbouleh salad
by Chef Julie Simon, Thomas Hill Organics

This Lebanese salad is loaded with fresh herbs!

Serves 4
- 1 cup of bulgur wheat
- 2 bunches of Italian parsley
- 1 bunch of mint
- 2 lemons, maybe 3
- 1/4 cup roasted pistachios
- ½ cup dates
- 2 English cucumbers
- 3 tablespoons extra virgin olive oil
- Sea salt and fresh pepper

- Soak and cover the bulgur in hot water for about 30 minutes, it will swell, and should be al dente at this point but not crunchy.

- In the meantime, chop all your herbs (no stems).

- Dice the cucumbers, slice the dates lengthwise, into 4-6 pieces, give a rough chop to the pistachios, juice and zest the lemons.

- Get back to the bulgur wheat, add olive oil, lemon juice & zest, stir, salt and cracked pepper, fold in the cucumber, dates, add a pinch more salt, stir, add the herbs. Re-season if needed.

- Add the pistachio when you are ready to serve so they remain crunchy.

barley salad by Chef Michael Foley, Chef's Table Catering

The pearl barley and fruit with a nice acid level in the vinaigrette make this a nice salad to pair with wine. You can adapt the recipe to fit the season by using seasonal fruits and vegetables.

Yield
- 1 cup Pearl barley
- 1 small can mandarin orange segments
- 1 cup butternut squash, peeled and diced small
- ½ cup sun dried blueberries
- As needed Orange-Mango Vinaigrette
- ½ teaspoon kosher salt
- ½ clove of garlic

Orange-Mango Vinaigrette
- 3 ounces olive oil
- 2 ounces Champagne vinegar
- ½ teaspoon fine chopped garlic
- ¼ teaspoon fine chopped thyme
- ½ teaspoon fresh Italian Parsley chopped fine
- 1 tablespoon mango puree
- 2 tablespoons orange juice
- Salt and Pepper to taste

- Mix all vinaigrette ingredients together and reserve until needed.

- Mix the pearl barley, salt and garlic together. Cover with water and bring to a boil over high heat. Reduce heat to medium and stirring occasionally, cook barley until tender approximately 30 minutes. Strain off the water and rinse under cool water until cool. This will wash away any excess starch from the barley. Remove the garlic clove.

- Add the squash to a pot of boiling water cooking until just tender. Approximately 5 minutes, cool immediately. Toss all ingredients together using enough vinaigrette to coat but not drown.

eat this with...
Adelaida Cellars Grenache Blanc
Pear Valley Our Daily White
Penman Springs Dry Humour
Pomar Junction Viognier
Robert Hall Orange Muscat
Tablas Creek Côtes de Tablas Blanc

mixed shellfish and couscous salad by Brigit Binns

This Mixed Shellfish and Couscous Salad with Meyer Lemon and Extra-Virgin Olive Oil Vinaigrette served on a big platter, family-style, makes an impressive and colourful center-piece. Take advantage of the luminously fresh seafood here on the central coast -- and for an added touch of Paso, use a high quality Paso Robles olive oil.

Serves 6

1 cup low-sodium chicken stock
2 tablespoons medium-dry white wine
1 tablespoon extra-virgin olive oil
1 tablespoon white wine vinegar
3/4 cup instant couscous
3/4 cup cooked bay shrimp
¾ cup cooked bay scallops
¼ cup finely chopped red onion
2 tablespoons capers, rinsed, drained, and chopped

Grated zest of two Meyer lemons
1 tablespoon fresh lemon juice
2 tablespoons finely chopped flat-leaf parsley
1/2 teaspoon sea salt
Freshly ground black pepper
1 small basket cherry tomatoes, halved
½ cup thawed frozen peas (optional)
Extra-virgin olive oil, for drizzling
Sprigs of fresh parsley, for garnish

- Bring the chicken stock, wine, olive oil, and vinegar to a boil and remove from the heat. Place the couscous in a metal mixing bowl and pour the hot liquid over the top. Cover the bowl and let stand for 5 minutes, then fluff with a fork to separate the grains. Stir in the shrimp, scallops, red onion, capers, lemon zest and juice, parsley, salt, and a generous amount of black pepper. Chill the mixture for at least 1 and up to 3 hours.

- Twenty minutes before serving, remove from the refrigerator and bring to room temperature. Taste for seasoning, then mound the mixture on a small platter and surround with the tomatoes and thawed peas (if using). Drizzle with additional extra-virgin olive oil, garnish with sprigs of parsley, and serve.

eat this with...

Caliza Kissin' Cousins
Caliza Pink
Clavo Viognier
Graveyard Pink
Grey Wolf Viognier
Pear Valley Albariño
Red Soles Viognier
Silver Horse Albariño

field mache with shitake bacon by Chef Charles D. Paladin Wayne

Salad of Field Mache with Candied Garlic and Shitake Bacon
Feta Cheese, Baby Heirloom Tomatoes and Banyuls Sherry Vinaigrette

Serves 10

Candied Garlic
1 cup Sugar
1 cup Chardonnay
1 cup peeled Fresh Garlic cloves ends trimmed

- In a sauce pan dissolve the sugar in the wine and add the garlic cloves. Bring to a slow rolling boil and watch for the cloves to become translucent and lightly tan colored. Set aside to cool. Can be stored in refrigerator for up to 6 months.

Pancetta Bacon Crisp
10 slices thin sliced pancetta

- Heat oven to 300f.
- Place Pancetta onto parchment and top with another parchment, bake until crisp.

Garlic Syrup and Sherry Vinaigrette
½ cup candied garlic (reserve syrup)
1/8 cup reserved candied garlic syrup
1/8 cup Rioja Spanish Sherry Vinegar
1/4 cup Extra Virgin Olive Oil
½ tsp salt
½ tsp pepper

- Place all ingredients into a blender to combine.

Salad
12 ounces Mache greens
1 cup baby heirloom tomatoes cut in half
½ cup sheep feta crumbled
¼ cup dressing
1 slice Pancetta Crisp

- In a non- reactive salad bowl toss Mache with dressing. Add tomatoes, garlic, feta, and Shitake Bacon. Plate the salad then the tomatoes, top with Garlic and Feta. Top with Pancetta Crisp and Serve.

eat this with...
Broken Earth Quadrant Gold

niçoise salad with seared tuna by Chef Natalie Dorris

The classic French salad is given a modern twist with seared yellow fin "Ahi" tuna standing in for the traditional canned albacore. Mixed greens can be substituted for the baby spinach.

Serves 4

6 ounce baby spinach
8-10 kalamata olives, halved
8-10 grape tomatoes, halved
4 ounces haricot vert, steamed and chilled
2 red potato, cooked and small diced
¼ red onion, thinly sliced
2 eggs, hard boiled, sliced in half
8 ounces yellowfin "Ahi" tuna steak
Salt & Pepper

Balsamic Vinaigrette
¼ cup balsamic vinegar
1 garlic clove, minced
1 teaspoon sugar
½ teaspoon Dijon mustard
½ teaspoon salt
½ teaspoon pepper
¾ cup extra virgin olive oil

- Season Ahi steak with salt and fresh ground pepper. Heat a small non-stick skillet to medium-high. Spray the pan with non-stick spray or a few drops of olive oil. Sear the tuna steak for 3-4 minutes on each side until golden on the outside, but with a cold, red center. Let rest for one minute then thinly slice.

- In a small bowl, whisk balsamic, garlic, sugar, mustard, salt and pepper until blended. Pour in oil a little at a time, whisking continually. Taste and adjust seasoning.

- In a large bowl, toss baby spinach in about ¼ cup of dressing. Lightly coat the leaves with dressing without over saturating them. Mound the spinach onto four chilled plates. Divide the olives, tomatoes, green beans, potato, red onion, and hard- boiled egg between all four plates. Placing neatly on top of the spinach, top each salad with about 2 ounces of sliced tuna. Drizzle extra dressing on top of the plate if desired.

eat this with...
Halter Ranch Sauvignon Blanc
Hug Rosé
JUSTIN Sauvignon Blanc
Pomar Junction "Brooster"
Shale Oak Albariño
Tablas Creek Vermentino
Vina Robles Verdelho

insalata alle-pia by Alle-Pia Fine Cured Meats

Each small batch of Alle-Pia salami is created with love by the talented Antonio Varia, Chef and Owner of Buona Tavola Restaurants in Paso Robles and San Luis Obispo. You will taste this devotion with each slice of Alle-Pia artisan salami you enjoy with family and friends. The salami really makes this salad unique.

Serves 4

Alle-Pia Sopressa Salami (or any Alle-Pia salami)
Baby arugula
Kalamata olives (pitted)
Sun-dried tomatoes (drained)
1 grapefruit
Extra virgin olive oil
Parmesan cheese

- Slice and peel the Alle-Pia Salami. Cut the slices in half. Peel the grapefruit and cut the wedges in sections. In a large bowl, mix the baby Arugula, Kalamata olives, sun-dried tomatoes, grapefruit sections and Alle-Pia Salami.

- Drizzle extra virgin olive oil over the mix to coat.

- Serve on 4 individual plates and top with shaved petals of parmesan cheese.

eat this with...

Eberle Barbera
J. Lohr Pinot Noir
Pear Valley Malbec
Ranchita Canyon Serenata
Nine Sangiouvese
Opolo Barbera
Shale Oak Petite Sirah
Still Waters Malbec
Wildhorse Pinot Noir
Windward Pinot Noir

wasabi salmon by Lisa Pretty

Wasabi peas can be found in most grocery stores or at Trader Joe's. Ground in a food processor they make the perfect spicy crush for a nice piece of salmon.

Serves 2
- **3 cups mixed greens**
- **1/2 cup chopped grape tomatoes**
- **1 + 3 tablespoons olive oil**
- **Juice of 1/2 lemon**
- **¾ cup wasabi peas**
- **2 salmon fillets (approximately 6 ounces each)**
- **Salt & pepper**

- In a medium bowl, mix greens, tomatoes, 1 tablespoon olive oil, lemon juice. Season with salt and pepper and toss again.

- Using a food processor, ground the wasabi peas until they are the consistency of bread crumbs. Brush the flesh side of each fillet with a little olive oil and coat with wasabi crumbs.

- Heat the remaining olive oil in a large frying pan and add 1 tablespoon of butter. Place the salmon flesh side down in the pan and cook over medium heat for approximately 4 minutes per side. Watch the fish carefully and reduce heat to medium-low if the oil/butter mixture gets too hot. You want to form a nice crust with a golden color.

- Divide the greens between two plates and top with salmon fillet.

eat this with...

Alto Colina Grenache
DAOU Merlot
J. Dusi Zinfandel
Halter Ranch Merlot
Kenneth Volk Merlot
Le Vigne Merlot
Robert Hall Merlot
Rotta Zinfandel
Tobin James Merlot
Zin Alley Zinfandel

chapter 4 - soups

chilled pea soup
by Chef Laurent Grangien, Bistro Laurent

Be sure to use only fresh green peas when making this recipe. The flavor of fresh peas, wine and cream combine to create a traditional cold soup.

Yield

1 pound fresh peas, shelled
1 medium yellow onion, chopped
½ cup dry white wine
1 cup cream
2 tablespoons butter
Salt and pepper, to taste

- Sautéed onion with butter in a medium sauce pan. Add peas, then white wine, continue to cook in an open pan until wine reduces by 1/3. Add water and cream. Cook slowly covered for 20 minutes. Season with salt and pepper.

- Blend soup in blender in batches. Chill down before serving.

eat this with...

Broken Earth Pinot Gris
Clavo Grenache Blanc
Halter Ranch Sauvignon Blanc
J Dusi Pinot Gris
JUSTIN Sauvignon Blanc
Mitchella Sauvignon Blanc
Pear Valley Grenache Blanc
Robert Hall Sauvignon Blanc
Tablas Creek Vermentino

chapter 2 - soups

gazpacho by Tablas Creek Vineyard

The end of the summer is tomato season throughout most of the United States, and there is no dish that tastes more like summer than gazpacho. This recipe, which, in the traditional Anadalucian style contains bread, is hearty enough for a light summer meal.

Serves 4-6

  4 slices country-style bread, about 1 inch thick
  4 small cucumbers, peeled, seeded and chopped
  4 pounds very ripe tomatoes, seeded and coarsely chopped
  2 cloves garlic, peeled and chopped
  1/2 cup sherry vinegar
  3/4 cup extra virgin olive oil
  1 cup water
  Salt, to taste

- Soak bread for 30 minutes in a small bowl in water to cover. Squeeze out moisture with your hands.

- Puree bread, cucumbers, tomatoes, garlic, vinegar, olive oil, and water with an immersion blender until very smooth. The soup should be fairly thin. Season to taste with salt.

- Chill gazpacho in refrigerator for at least two hours. Adjust seasonings and serve in individual glasses or soup bowls.

eat this with...
Tablas Creek Rosé

chapter 2 - soups

vichyssoise by Jason Moore

This cold, potato-leek soup is perfect on a hot summer day. Jason adds raw green onion and curry powder for a flavor spike and touch of color.

Serves 4-6

36 ounces chicken stock
1 russet potato peeled, chopped
1/2 stick butter
2 leek, chopped
1 golden onion, chopped
Sea salt, to taste
Fresh ground black pepper, to taste
Heavy cream
1 bunch green onion (for garnish)
Curry powder (for garnish)

eat this with...

Adelaida Version White
Red Soles Reserve Chardonnay
Halter Ranch Rosé
Robert Hall Chardonnay
Tablas Creek Rosé
Vina Robles White[4]

- Place half of the chicken stock in a medium sauce pan and bring to a boil. Add potatoes and cook over medium heat until they are tender (approximately 10 minutes)

- In a medium fry pan melt the butter. Sauté leeks and onions in butter taking care not to let the butter get too hot and brown. Remove from heat with onions are translucent.

- Transfer leeks, onion, potatoes and chicken stock to a large bowl, using immersion blender, blend until smooth. Use additional chicken stock to thin as necessary. Adjust seasoning with salt & pepper.

- Chill for at least two hours.

- Whisk in cream just prior to serving. Garnish with chopped green onion & curry powder.

CHEF'S PROFILE: *Chef Jacob Lovejoy*

Chef Jacob attended culinary school in Fresno and worked as the Executive Chef at the Carlton Hotel in Atascadero prior to taking the Chef position at the Cass Café.

He has made himself at home at Cass Winery and even tends his own garden to ensure fresh ingredients are only a couple of minutes away from his kitchen.

He enjoys pairing food with wine and his creative menu changes frequently. In addition to regular hours at the Cass Café, he also stays busy with Cass Catering.

puree of fagioli bean soup by Chef Jacob Lovejoy, Cass Café

Chef Jacob's puree of Fagioli bean soup with pancetta lardons topped with a Parmesan crisp makes a beautiful presentation

Serves 6

- 2 tablespoons butter
- 1 tablespoon olive oil
- 2 shallots, chopped
- 1 sage leaf
- 2 (15-ounce) cans cannellini beans, drained and rinsed
- 4 cups low-sodium chicken broth
- 4 cloves garlic, cut in 1/2
- 1/2 cup cream
- 1/2 teaspoon freshly ground black pepper
- ½ cup shredded Parmesan cheese
- ¼ cup pancetta or bacon, cubed and cooked off

- ◦ Preheat oven to 350F.

- ◦ Place a medium, heavy soup pot over medium heat. Add the butter, olive oil, and shallot. Cook, stirring occasionally, until the shallots are softened, about 5 minutes. Add the sage and beans, stir to combine. Add the stock and bring the mixture to a simmer. Add the garlic and simmer until the garlic is softened, about 10 minutes. Pour the soup into a large bowl. Carefully ladle 1/3 to 1/2 of the soup into a blender and puree until smooth. Be careful to hold the top of the blender tightly, as hot liquids expand when they are blended. Pour the blended soup back into the soup pan. Puree the remaining soup. Once all the soup is blended and back in the soup pan, add the cream and the pepper and stir.

- ◦ For the Parmesan crisps, spray a baking sheet with non-stick spray. Place several rows of cheese along the plate, 4 inches long, 1 inch wide, and 1/8 inch high. Place pan in the oven and bake for approximately 5 minutes, until cheese is melted and browning. Remove from oven and place on cooling rack immediately.

- ◦ Ladle the soup evenly into the serving bowls. Place a Parmesan crisp out of the top, and top with the lardons.

eat this with...

Cass Grenache

minestrone soup by Paul Ruberto, Pulcinella Wood-Fired Pizza

Paul Ruberto specializes in wood-fired pizza made following traditional Italian techniques. His catering busines; however, does far more than pizza pies. The minestrone soup recipe will fill your home with mouth watering aromas; you may have a difficult time getting your guests to leave!

Serves 12

¼ cup extra virgin olive oil

2 cups onion, ½" dice

2 cups carrots, peeled ½" dice

2 cups celery ½" dice

4 garlic cloves, minced

2 cups potato, ½" dice

8 ounces green beans, cut fresh or frozen

2 small zucchini, ½" dice

2 small yellow squash, ½" Dice

6 – 8 cups cabbage, medium chop

2 quarts each, chicken & vegetable broth

2 large cans crushed tomatoes

1 (15 ounce) can red kidney beans, drained & rinsed

1 (15oz) can white cannellini beans, drained & rinsed

1 cup small pasta, cooked al dente

1 bunch fresh spinach, washed & chopped

½ cup each, chopped fresh basil and Italian parsley

eat this with...
Eberle Sangiovese
Ranchita Canyon Sangiovese
Robert Hall Grenache

- In a large stock pot, heat the oil over medium flame. When very hot, add the onion, cook 4 minutes. Add the celery and carrots, cook 4 minutes. Add the garlic, cook 1 minute. Add the potatoes and fresh green beans cook 3 minutes. Add zucchini, yellow squash and cabbage, cook 2 minutes. Add beans, tomatoes, and broths. Bring to a boil and then reduce heat and simmer for 1 hour.

- Add 1 cup cooked small pasta. Add basil, spinach and Italian parsley, salt & pepper to taste.

- Serve this with freshly grated Romano cheese, & cracked black pepper.

french onion soup by Lisa Pretty

A perfect starter, or light meal, French onion soup with rich broth, thick bread and gooey cheese, is an easy soup to pair with wine. The soup goes well with whites and reds -- in fact the broth may be made with either.

Serves 6

- ¼ cup butter (1/2 stick)
- 4 large yellow onions, cut in half and sliced
- 2 teaspoons dried thyme
- 4 cups beef broth
- 1 cup dry white (or red) wine
- 2 tablespoons Worcestershire sauce
- 3 dried bay leaves
- Salt & pepper to taste
- ½ French baguette, sliced or cubed
- 1 cup grated Gruyere cheese

- Melt butter in a medium sauce pan. Add onions and thyme, stir to coat, then reduce heat to low. Allow the onions to cook slowly and caramelize, stir occasionally (approximately 45 minutes).

- Add beef stock, wine, Worcestershire sauce, bay leaves, salt and pepper. Increase heat, stir and bring to a boil. Reduce heat and simmer for 45 minutes. Remove and discard bay leaves.

- Place soup in oven proof bowls, place bread on top of soup and cover with grated cheese. Melt the cheese under a broiler. The cheese should just begin to brown.

- Serve in the hot soup bowl.

eat this with...

Adelaida Viognier
Caliza Syrah
Castoro Syrah
HammerSky Merlot
Le Vigna Merlot
Pear Valley Merlot
Robert Hall Viognier

chapter 2 - soups

hearty potato soup by Pat Lareau, travel-and-eat.blogspot.com

This hearty soup by Pat Lareau is like a lasagna soup. The soup is created in layers and topped with cheese. Be sure to use a bowl that is oven proof when you make this recipe.

Serves 4-6

1 eggplant, sliced 1/4' thick, length of eggplant
4 cups grated mixed Italian cheeses
1/2 loaf thin sliced country bread
2 large tomatoes, sliced
1 yellow onion, sliced thin and par boiled
1 fennel bulb, sliced thin and par boiled
Fresh basil, chiffonade
4 cups chicken stock (best if homemade)
1/4 cup chopped chorizo

- Preheat oven to 350F.

- Using a baking bowl with a wide top, layer bread, eggplant slices, fennel, tomato, chorizo, basil, cheese. Repeat layers

- Pour boiling HOT chicken stock over all, until liquid level is almost to the top. Crown with a third layer of bread and cheese.

- Bake in 350 oven until cheese is melted and golden on top - about 20-30 minutes. Each serving should have part of the lovely golden top.

eat this with...
Alta Colina Syrah
Caliza Syrah
Clayhouse Petite Sirah
Pear Vallery Charbono
Penman Springs Syrah
Pomar Junction Fiesta Red
Pretty-Smith Cabernet Sauvignon
Ranchita Canyon Sangiovese
Robert Hall Syrah

oyster saffron chowder by Chef Andre Averseng, Paso Terra Seafood

The pinch of saffron gives this chowder a pretty color and delightful aroma.

Serves 6

- 4 slices bacon, chopped
- 2 tablespoons olive oil
- 1 small onion diced
- 1 rib celery, sliced thinly
- 1 carrot, diced
- ½ red bell pepper, diced
- 2 cloves garlic, diced
- Salt, pepper and cayenne, to taste
- 2 pinches saffron
- 1 cup white wine
- 3 medium diced potatoes
- 30 shucked oysters
- 2 cups fish stock
- 3 cups cream
- 2 tablespoons chives, chopped
- 1 tablespoon fresh parsley, chopped

- Sauté bacon in a large frying pan. Remove from pan and reserve for later use.

- Add olive oil, onion, celery, carrot and bell pepper to the pan and sweat the vegetables until tender. Add garlic, saffron, salt, pepper and cayenne. Add white wine and potato, cook for 5 minutes. Add oyster, stock, and cream and cook for 10 minutes.

- Serve in bowls garnished with with bacon, chives and parsley.

eat this with...
Graveyard Chardonnay
J. Lohr Riesling
Pear Valley Our Daily White
Penman Springs Dry Humour
Tablas Creek Côtes de Tablas Blanc

sweet potato soup by Lisa Pretty

*A nice bowl of warm soup for lunch or as a start to a multi course dinner is very welcoming.
This recipe will warm your guests' hearts and their bellies too!*

Serves 4

2 tablespoons olive oil

2 medium leeks, white parts thinly sliced

3 tablespoons tomato based chili paste

2 cloves of garlic, minced

1 teaspoon ground cumin

1 teaspoon ground turmeric

2 medium sweet potatoes, peeled and cut into 1" cubes

5 cups chicken stock

2 cups chopped kale leaves

½ cup chopped cashews

eat this with...

J. Dusi Fiorento

J. Lohr Chardonnay

Kukkula Sisu

LXV Crimson Jewel

Pear Valley Tom's Oak Chardonnay

Penman Springs Merlot

Robert Hall Grenache

SummerWood Grenache

- In a large pot eat the oil and sauté the leeks. Stir in tomato paste, garlic, cumin and turmeric. Cook for 1 minute and add stock and sweet potatoes. Bring to a boil then reduce heat to simmer for 20-25 minutes, or until potatoes are tender.

- Remove from heat and blend with an immersion blender. Return to heat and bring to a boil. Add kale and stir. Simmer for 5 additional minutes.

- Place soup in bowls and top with chopped cashews.

black bean soup by Chef Jeffry Wiesinger, Jeffry's Catering

Ancho Chili-Black Bean Soup with Crispy Spanish Chorizo

Serves 8

1/3 cup olive oil + 1 teaspoon for chorizo
2 medium red onions, small diced
1 medium red bell pepper, small diced
1 medium green bell pepper, small diced
3 medium Roma tomatoes, deseeded & diced
6 garlic cloves, finely minced
3 dried Ancho chilies, soaked, deseeded & chopped
2 tablespoons kosher salt
1 tablespoon ground black pepper

1 tablespoon ground cumin
1 lime, zested & juiced
1-16 ounces dried black beans
8 cups water or stock
4 ounces Spanish chorizo, small diced
½ cup plain Greek yogurt
½ cup sour cream
1 lime, zested & juiced
2 tablespoons fresh cilantro leaves, chopped

- Soak beans in water overnight and drain.

- Heat olive oil in a medium size soup pot over medium-high heat. Add onions & peppers and sauté until soft, about 8 minutes. Add garlic, Ancho chilies & tomatoes; continue to sauté for an additional 7 minutes. Add presoaked black beans & water (or stock) stir to combine. Turn heat to medium-low, cover & cook for 1-2 hours at a slow simmer until beans are very tender. Check beans for tenderness & season with salt, pepper, cumin, lime juice & lime zest. Remove 2 cups of bean mixture and puree in a blender until smooth. Return puree to soup, stir & check for seasoning.

- In a medium sauté pan, heat 1 teaspoon olive oil & fry chorizo for 3-4 minutes until crispy. Drain chorizo on paper towel & set aside

- Combine Greek yogurt, sour cream, lime juice & zest.

- Ladle soup into bowls and spoon a dollop of lime-cream mixture into each bowl. Top with a pinch of chopped cilantro & crispy chorizo.

eat this with...
Derby Pinot Noir
J. Dusi Carignane
Pear Valley Aglianico
PULL CdR

chapter 5 - entrées

prosciutto wrapped swordfish by Chef Andre, Paso Terra Seafood

Chef Andres wraps his swordfish in prosciutto and tops with a wine reduction sauce.

Serves 8
- 24 oz swordfish cut into 3 oz portions
- 4 slices prosciutto cut in half lengthwise
- 8 purple potatoes
- 4 ounces yellow onion, sliced
- 2 cloves garlic, minced
- Salt & pepper, to taste
- 2 tablespoons olive oil
- 1 ounce butter

Reduction Sauce
- ½ bottle of Syrah
- 6 ounces brown sugar
- Salt and pepper, to taste

- Cook down in sauce pan. When reduced by 2/3 remove from head and let cool. Sauce will continue to thicken and become a glaze for fish.

- Wrap fish with prosciutto and reserve.
- Sauté sliced potatoes in oil and butter for 5 minutes. Add onion and garlic and cook until onions are soft. Add salt and pepper. Bake in 350 degree oven for 40 minutes.
- Sauté fish in olive oil.
- Divide potatoes across 8 plates. Top with fish. Brush fish with reduction sauce to form a glaze.

eat this with...

Eberle Syrah
Graveyard Estate Syrah
J. Dusi Syrah La Casita
Kukkula Sisu
Robert Hall Syrah

fish potato casserole by Lisa Pretty

Fish and potato based casserole is my idea of inexpensive comfort food. The secret to this recipe is to start with good potatoes — I like the small red skin or baby Yukon Golds. The smaller potatoes seem to have a better texture and fresher flavor which hold up during roasting.

Serves 4

- 2 tablespoons olive oil
- 1 large scallion, halved and sliced
- 2 celery stocks, chopped
- 1 large carrot, chopped
- 4 cups chopped baby potatoes
- 1 can clams (15 ounces)
- 8 ounce clam juice
- 2 cups white wine
- 6 ounces cod, cut into 1 inch cubes
- 1 large tomato, chopped
- 1 tablespoon dried thyme
- 1 teaspoon dried pepper flakes
- ¼ cup fresh basil leaves, chopped
- Salt and pepper to taste

eat this with...

Asuncion Ridge Pinot Noir
Pretty-Smith Palette de Rouge
Wild Horse Pinot Noir
Windward Pinot Noir

- Preheat oven to 400F

- Heat olive oil on the stove top in a casserole dish that is both stove top and oven proof. Sauté scallions, celery and carrot for approximately 5 minutes. Add the potatoes and continue to sauté for an additional 5 minutes. Add the remaining ingredients and stir to mix all ingredients.

- Place casserole dish in oven and roast at 400F for 40 minutes.

chapter 5 - entrées

grilled halibut by Lisa Pretty

A good quality piece of meaty fish is required for this recipe -- I prefer halibut; however, seabass and swordfish are other good choices. If you do not have infused vinegar, simply zest an orange and soak it in plain white wine vinegar for 30 minutes.

Serves 2

1 large halibut steak cut in half
1 teaspoon olive oil
Sea salt, to taste

Sauce

½ cup white wine vinegar infused with orange zest
¼ cup soy sauce
¼ cup fresh orange juice
1 tablespoon dried thyme
¼ teaspoon cayenne pepper
1 tablespoon brown sugar

- In a small sauce pan bring vinegar, soy sauce, orange juice, thyme and pepper to a boil. Reduce heat and simmer until sauce reduces by half its volume, stir occasionally. Stir in brown sugar and simmer for an additional 5 minutes.

- Rub halibut with olive oil, sprinkle with sea salt and grill over medium heat. I prefer to use a fish basket on the grill to keep the fish from sticking and also give the fish those perfect grill marks. Grill for approximately 3 minutes on each side (grilling time will depend on the thickness of the halibut steak). Be sure not to overcook.

- Serve halibut steak with sauce drizzled on top.

eat this with...

Caliza Sidekick
Pear Valley Chardonnay
Polmar Junction Viognier
Robert Hall Grenache Blanc

curry tilapia by Lisa Pretty

Curried peppers, served over a bed of baby spinach topped with tilapia, then drizzled with a little curry sauce pairs well with white wines exhibiting tropical notes, slight roundness and lingering acidity.

Serves 4
- **2 tablespoons olive oil**
- **2 red bell peppers, sliced**
- **2 poblano peppers, sliced**
- **1 can light coconut milk**
- **1 tablespoon Hot Madras Curry Powder**
- **1 teaspoon cayenne pepper**
- **½ cup chopped fresh basil**
- **4 tilapia fillets**
- **1 teaspoon dried thyme**
- **Salt & pepper, to taste**
- **4 cups fresh baby spinach**
- **4 tilapia fillets**

eat this with...
Clavo Vermentino
JUSTIN Rosé
Halter Ranch Rosé
LXV Heartnote Rosé
Pear Valley Merlot
Robert Hall Viognier
Shale Oak Rosé

- In a large fry pan heat 1 tablespoon of olive oil and sauté the peppers until they start to soften. Add the coconut milk, curry powder and cayenne pepper. Bring to a slow boil then reduce to simmer, stirring occasionally.

- While the peppers simmer, heat the remaining olive oil in another frying pan. Sprinkle thyme, salt and pepper on the tilapia and cook in the heated pan for approximately 2 minutes per side.

- Add the chopped basil to the peppers and adjust seasoning if required. Remove from heat and place a heaping serving over a plate of spinach. Place the fish on top and drizzle with a little of the curry sauce from the pan.

grilled game hens provencal by Brigit Binns

Game hens are perfectly sized for individual servings—thus removing the messy necessity of carving a chicken on a picnic—but they can be lacking in flavor. This recipe radically increases the flavor profile by briefly brining the little birds, then add classic South-of-France ingredients: brine-cured olives, rosemary, and tangy hints of citrus.

Serves 6

Brine:

2 quarts cold water

½ cup kosher or coarse sea salt

¼ cup granulated sugar

Several branches of fresh thyme & rosemary

2 tablespoons whole black peppercorns

3 Cornish game hens, about 1 ½ pounds each

1/3 cup finely chopped fresh rosemary

6 cloves garlic, finely chopped

Finely grated zest of 1 lemon

1 tablespoon of fresh lemon juice

Finely grated zest of 1 orange

1 tablespoon fresh orange juice

1/4 cup calamata olives , pitted and minced

1 teaspoon coarsely ground black pepper

2 tablespoons extra-virgin olive oil

1 orange, cut into slices, for serving

Sprigs of rosemary, for serving

1 cup pitted calamata olives, for serving

- For the brine: In a small saucepan, warm 2 cups of the water over medium heat. Remove from the heat and stir in the salt and sugar until completely dissolved. Transfer the mixture to a tall, nonreactive container that will fit into your refrigerator (a crock works well, or a food-service bucket/tupperware). Add the remaining water, herb branches, and peppercorns. Remove the wishbone from between the top of the breasts with a small, sharp knife (this makes it much easier to carve). Remove the backbone by cutting along either side with sharp kitchen shears and, with the hens breast side up, push down to flatten with the palm of your hand, breaking some of the rib bones. Repeat with the remaining hens and immerse them in the brine. Refrigerate for at least 6 hours, and up to overnight if desired.

- Lift the hens from the brine and pat dry thoroughly all over with paper towels.

- In a small bowl, make a paste with the rosemary, garlic, lemon zest and juice, orange zest and juice, minced olives, pepper, and olive oil. Smear this paste all over both sides of the halved hens, gently loosening the skin of the breasts and thighs to push some of the paste underneath (be careful not to tear the skin).

- Prepare a charcoal or gas grill for indirect grilling over medium heat. Clean and oil the grill grate to prevent sticking, if necessary, and place a drip pan between the coals, under the entire center of the grate.

- Grill, the hens skin side up with the grill closed for 12 minutes without moving them around (this will stop them from sticking). Turn over and grill for 15 to 20 minutes more, turning again once or twice if desired, until the juices from the thigh run clear and the internal temperature of the thigh is 160°F. Transfer to a clean platter and tent loosely with foil. Let rest for 10 minutes, then serve each half-hen with lemon wedges, a sprig or two of rosemary, and a few olives.

eat this with...

Caliza Azimuth
Eberle Chardonnay
Halter Ranch Rosé
Kukkula Sisu
Pear Valley Inspiration
Ranchita Canyon
Robert Hall Cuvée de Robles
Shale Oak Syrah
Tablas Creek Rosé

chicken saltimbocca by Chef Jacob Lovejoy, Cass Café

*Warm bruschetta, fennel risotto, chef's garden squash
with blossoms in brown butter*

Serves 6

For the Chicken:
6 (3-ounce) chicken cutlets, pounded flat
Salt and freshly ground black pepper
6 paper-thin slices prosciutto
10 fresh sage leaves
½ cup shredded provolone cheese
3 tablespoons olive oil

~ Preheat oven to 375 degrees. Place the chicken cutlets flat on the work surface. Sprinkle the chicken with salt and pepper. Lay 1 slice of prosciutto atop each chicken cutlet. Arrange an even, thin layer of cheese atop the prosciutto slices, and sprinkle it with the sage evenly over each. Beginning at the short tapered end, roll up each chicken cutlet as for a jelly roll. Secure with a toothpick. Heat the 2 tablespoons of oil in a heavy large skillet over high heat. Add the chicken and cook just until golden brown, about 2 minutes per side. Remove from pan and arrange in a baking dish. Bake until chicken is cooked through, approximately 12 minutes.

For the warm bruschetta:
6 or 7 ripe plum tomatoes,
2 cloves garlic, minced
2 tbsp extra virgin olive oil
1 teaspoon white balsamic vinegar
6-8 fresh basil leaves, chiffonade
Salt and freshly ground black pepper to taste

~ Seed and dice tomatoes into ¼ inch cubes.

~ Combine all ingredients and warm in medium saucepan over low heat. Spoon over chicken when plating.

For the fennel risotto:
  6 cups chicken broth
  1 cup dry white wine
  2 tablespoons unsalted butter
  ½ cup finely chopped onion
  ½ cup finely chopped fennel bulb (anise)
  Kosher salt and freshly ground black pepper
  2 cups Arborio rice
  1/2 cup grated Parmesan
  1 teaspoon grated lemon zest
  1/2 teaspoon freshly grated nutmeg

- In a medium saucepan with a lid, combine chicken broth and white wine and heat just to simmering. Keep warm.

- In a large 3 to 4-quart heavy saucepan over medium heat, melt the butter. Add the onions, fennel, and a pinch of salt and sweat until translucent, about 5 minutes. Add the rice and stir. Cook for 3 to 5 minutes or until the grains are translucent around the edges. Be careful not to allow the grains or the onions to brown. Reduce the heat to low. Add enough of the wine and chicken stock just to cover the top of the rice. Stir or move the pan often, until the liquid is completely absorbed into rice.

- Once absorbed, add enough liquid just to cover the rice and continue stirring or moving as before. There should be just enough liquid left to repeat 1 more time. It should take approximately 35 to 40 minutes for all of the liquid to be absorbed. After the last addition and absorption of liquid, remove from the heat and stir in the Parmesan, lemon zest, and nutmeg. Taste and season, to taste, with salt and freshly ground black pepper.

eat this with...
Cass Rockin' One Red

chicken kiev by Lisa Pretty

The real trick to creating a good Chicken Kiev is sealing the herb butter in the center. The herb butter should be hard and the chicken needs to be wrapped around the butter with no places for the butter to seep out while it cooks. There is nothing like cutting into the center and having that ooze of fragrant herb butter burst from the center.

Serves 4

- 1 stick of butter
- 2 tablespoons chopped fresh tarragon
- 1 tablespoon chopped fresh chives
- 4 skinless, boneless chicken breasts
- 1 cup flour
- 1 teaspoon salt
- 1 teaspoon pepper
- 1 teaspoon dried thyme
- 2 eggs, beaten
- 1 1/2 cups Panko bread crumbs
- 2 tablespoons olive oil

eat this with...

Eberle Chardonnay
J. Lohr Chardonnay
Pear Valley Tom's Oak Chardonnay
Pomar Junction Chardonnay
Robert Hall Chardonnay

- Melt butter in a small sauce pan. Stir fresh herbs into the hot butter and let set until it cools and the herbs flavor the butter. Pour into small container and place in the refrigerator to harden for at least 1 hour (this can be done the day before).

- Place each chicken breast between wax paper and pound until it is approximately ¼ inch thick. Place one third of the hard butter in the center of each breast. Tuck the sides around the butter and roll. Use a toothpick to keep ends tightly wrapped.

- Prepare three large bowls for the breading process. In the first, mix together the flour, salt, pepper and thyme. In the second place the beaten eggs. The third should contain the Panko crumbs. Coast each breast by rolling first in the flour, then the egg, and finally the bread crumbs. Place the coated breasts on a plate in the refrigerator for 1 hour. This will help the chicken from a seal with the butter in the center.

- Preheat oven to 375F. Heat olive oil in a large, non-stick frying pan. Over high heat, place each breast in one at a time and brown on all sides. Place the golden brown breasts in a non-stick baking pan and place in the oven. Bake for 20-30 minutes.

herb roasted chicken by Chef Kelly Wangard, SummerWood Inn

This Olive oil & Herb Roasted Chicken with garlic Marsala jus by Chef Kelly is perfect in the Fall.

Serves 4

4 6-8 ounce portions of Airline chicken breast
1 teaspoon cracked black pepper
Small bunch of fresh oregano, chopped
Small bunch of fresh parsley, chopped
Small bunch of fresh tarragon, chopped
1 teaspoon fennel seed
¼ teaspoon red chili flakes
2 cups SummerWood Viognier
1 cup extra virgin olive oil

Sauce

1 tablespoon olive oil
2 cups sliced crimini mushrooms
4 cloves garlic, chopped fine
1 cup marsala wine
½ cup cream
1 stick butter
1 teaspoon salt

- Combine pepper, herbs, chili flakes, wine and oil. Cover chicken with marinade. Marinate for 1 hour.

- Heat a large sauté pan to high heat. Add in 3 tablespoons olive oil when the pan is hot. Carefully add the chicken breast skin side down, throw out the marinade. Allow the chicken to get golden brown, this should take about 3-5 minutes and then turn over. Place the pan in the oven and cook for 10 minutes or until 155 degrees internally. Allow the chicken to rest for 5 minutes.

- Create Sauce: In a sauce pan, add olive oil, garlic and mushrooms cook for 2-3 minutes or until garlic is light brown. Carefully add the marsala. Add cream. Allow to cook for 7-10 minutes or it looks like it is reduced by half. Remove from heat and add the butter with a whisk.

- Slice the chicken and serve with the mushroom sauce, vegetables or rice.

eat this with...
SummerWood Cabernet Sauvignon

chicken vindaloo by Chef Thomas Drahos, Avant-Garde Catering

Vindaloo is a hot and spicy dish. Chef Thomas uses a number of spices in this fragrant sauce.

Serves 6

2 pounds chicken breast
Salt and pepper to taste
4 tablespoons olive oil
1 teaspoon coriander seed
1 teaspoon cardamom seed ground
3 each pepper corns
1 teaspoon ground cloves
1 tablespoon chili powder
1 teaspoon cinnamon
1 teaspoon fenugreek ground

½ knob ginger, minced
1 teaspoon cumin
1 tablespoon dry mustard
2 cloves garlic, finely chopped
1 cup vinegar
5 tablespoons olive oil
2 onions, diced small
4 bay leaves
1 1/4 cups water
Salt and pepper, to taste
½ pound butter

- Preheat oven to 400F.

- Heat a medium sauté pan over high heat. Add some olive oil to coat the pan, gently placing chicken breast skin down on to oil pressing to make sure all the surface has made contact. Sear for five minutes or until golden brown. Remove and place on a sheet pan. Repeat until all chicken is seared. Bake until internal temperature reaches 160F. Rest for three minutes and then slice and serve.

- Heat a medium sauce pot over high heat. Put all remaining ingredients except the chicken water, vinegar and butter into the pot and cook over high heat until it begins to smoke to release all essential oils. Add liquid and stir until hot. Blend in a blender on high speed, adding butter one cube at a time to create a silky sauce. Keep hot until needed.

- To plate, place a spoon full of vindaloo sauce on large plate using your spoon, drag through it and place sliced chicken on top.

eat this with...
Castoro Gewurztraminer
Eos Gewurztraminer
J. Lohr Gewurztraminer
LXV Rising Temp
Pear Valley Charbono

chicken biryani by Neeta Mittal, LXV Wines

Biryani is derived from the Farsi word 'Birian'. Based on the name, and cooking style (Dum), it probably originated in Persia and/or Arabia. According to one legend, Mumtaz Mahal, the beauty who sleeps in Taj Mahal, concocted this dish as a "complete meal" to feed the army.

Serves 8

- 1.5 pounds chicken thighs
- 1 cup plain yogurt
- 2 teaspoons turmeric
- 2 teaspoons fennel seeds
- 2 teaspoons cumin seeds
- 1 teaspoon coriander seeds
- 3 tablespoons vegetable oil
- 4 large onions, finely sliced
- 2 teaspoons garlic, finely chopped
- 1 tablespoon ginger, finely chopped
- 2 teaspoon cayenne pepper
- 2 medium tomatoes, finely chopped
- 1 teaspoon garam masala
- 3 cups Basmati rice
- 1 stick cinnamon
- 5 cloves

- Cut chicken into 2 inch cubes and marinate with yogurt, salt and turmeric for at least 3 hours. Soak the rice for an hour.

- In a thick bottom skillet, sauté fennel, cumin and coriander seeds. Crush them in a mortar pestle and keep aside. Heat oil in the skillet. Add the sliced onions and fry 30 minutes until they are dark brown. Add the ginger and garlic. Sauté until the garlic turns pale brown. Add cayenne pepper, and sauté for a few seconds then add tomatoes and fry until the oil leaves the mix.

- Add the marinated chicken and the crushed spices, cover the skillet with a heavy lid and cook over low flame, mixing the ingredients gently every few minutes. When the chicken is almost done, mix the garam masala, and cook uncovered for a few minutes to reduce the gravy.

- Boil the rice on a very high flame along with the cinnamon and cloves. Add pinch of salt and dash of oil. When the rice is par boiled, drain the water and add it gently on top of the chicken, cover with the heavy lid again, and put on low heat for at least 45 minutes.

> **eat this with...**
> **LXV Heart Note**

italian sausage and beans by Il Cortile Ristorante

This Hot Italian Sausage with Cannellini Beans makes can be served as an entrée or in smaller portions as a first course. The combination of beans and sausage is an Italian classic.

Yield
1 cup of cannellini beans
2 pieces of hot Italian Sausage
1 cup fresh chopped tomatoes
1/2 chopped fresh basil
1 cup white wine
Salt to taste
Fresh parsley (for garnish)

- Cook the cannellini beans in water for about 45 minutes until al dente.

- Brown the Italian Sausage in a fry pan and cook until just done. Take the sausage and slice it on a diagonal. Put back in the pan and heat. Add the white wine and let reduce about 3 – 5 minutes. Add the tomatoes and let simmer. Add the cannellini beans and continue to cook. Salt to taste. Add the basil and cook for a few more minutes.

- Plate and sprinkle with fresh parsley.

eat this with...

Adelaida Syrah
Aron Hill Primitivo
Caliza Syrah
J. Lohr Estates South Ridge Syrah
Oso Libre Syrah
Pear Valley Syrah
Ranchita Canyon Sangiovese
Robert Hall Syrah
Tobin James Primitivo

chapter 5 - entrées

grilled duck breast by Ian McPhee, McPhee's Grill

Grilled Duck Breast with plum- poblano chile chutney. Ian adds a little kick to his grilled duck breast with this tasty chutney.

Serves 4

- 4 boneless duck breast
- 3 tablespoons olive oil
- ½ cup diced red onion
- 1 tablespoon minced garlic
- 1 poblano chile, roasted, peeled and diced
- 1 jalapeno chile, roasted, peeled and diced
- 2 cups diced fresh plums
- ¼ cup white balsamic vinegar
- 2 tablespoons honey

- ❧ Duck Preparation: With sharp knife score the duck skin, careful not to cut into the meat. Score into diamond shape. When cooking this will help the fat release from under the skin. Cook the duck breast skin side down over a medium fire, watch as the fat cooks out you will have flare-ups, just move to another part of the grill. Cook till skin starts to get crispy, then flip over and cook a few minutes to finish. Remove to a plate and loosely cover with foil to rest for 10 minutes. Slice thin and fan onto dinner plate.

- ❧ Roasting peppers: Set peppers on grill or open stove flame and turn till the skin has blackened. Put in paper bag for 15 minutes to steam skin. Remove from bag and peel skin off the peppers.

- ❧ Chutney preparation: Heat olive oil in pan add onions and garlic cook for 2 minutes, don't let them brown. Add rest of ingredients and cook till it becomes syrupy. Let cool. This can be served cold or reheated.

CHEF's PROFILE: Cook Ian McPhee

Ian may call himself a cook; however, he is one of the most talented restaurant chefs in the Central Coast. McPhee's Grill opened in 1994 in beautiful downtown Templeton.

June and Ian McPhee's motto is "great food and great service". They feature seasonal menus using the finest foods.

eat this with...

J. Lohr Merlot
Pear Valley Merlot
PULL Merlot
Ranchita Canyon Merlot
Robert Hall Cabernet Sauvignon

pan roasted duck breast by Chef Ryan Swarthout

Pan Roasted Duck Breast with Wild Mushroom Risotto and Dried Cherry Sauce

Serves 4

Duck:
- 4 each duck breast, trimmed and scored
- Salt and pepper
- 1 T olive oil

Risotto:
- 4 tablespoons olive oil
- 2 gloves garlic, chopped
- 1 pounds assorted mushrooms, shiitake, crimini and oyster, sliced
- 1 medium yellow onion, small dice
- 2 cups Arborio Rice
- 2 cups white wine
- 6 to 7 cups chicken stock
- 2 tablespoons butter
- ½ cup parmesan, grated
- ¼ cup chives, chopped

Sauce:
- 1 cup dried cherries
- 1 cup red wine
- 2 cups beef stock

eat this with...
Penman Springs Syrah

- Duck: Place the duck breast on a cutting board, using a knife cut one inch slices into the skin but not all the way through. This will aid in cooking the breast evenly. This is called scoring the duck breast. Heat the oil in a large sauté pan over medium heat. Place skin side down first and cook for 5 minutes. Turn and continue to cook for 2 more minutes. Remove the sauté pan from heat and let the duck rest before serving.

- Risotto: Heat the oil in a heavy bottom large sauce pot over medium heat. Add the chopped garlic and onions and cook until translucent. Add the sliced assorted mushrooms and cook until tender. Add the Arborio rice and stir a couple of times to coat the rice 2-3 minutes. Deglaze the rice with the white wine, continuing to stir until the wine is absorbed. Add enough stock to cover rice and continue to stir until stock is absorbed. Repeat two more times. Add the butter, Parmesan and chives, stir until well combined.

- Sauce: Place all ingredients in a sauce pot and bring to a boil. After the alcohol cooks off 2-3 minutes reduce to a simmer, continue to cook for 10 minutes or reduced by half. Place everything in a blender and carefully puree.

- Assembly: Slice duck breast into 5-7 slices. Spoon ¼ – ½ cup into bowl, place slice duck on top of the risotto and drizzle sauce on top and around duck.

turkey loaf by Lisa Pretty

Lean ground turkey and vegetables makes this loaf a little healthier than the classic meat loaf.

Serves 6

1 tablespoon olive oil
1 cup chopped onions
2 cloves garlic, chopped
1 cup chopped carrots
1 cup chopped celery
1 cup vegetable stock
1 tablespoon tomato paste
1 teaspoon dried thyme
¼ cup chopped fresh parsley
1 tablespoon Worcestershire sauce
Salt & pepper, to taste
1 pound ground turkey
2 eggs, beaten
1 cup whole wheat bread crumbs
1/3 cup tomato based chili sauce

eat this with...
Austin Hope Grenache
J. Lohr Merlot
JUSTIN Justification
SummerWood Merlot
Pear Valley Cabernet Franc
Penman Springs Rosé
Robert Hall Grenache

- Pre-heat oven to 350F

- Heat olive oil in a medium frying pan. Add onions and garlic, sauté for 3 minutes. Add carrots and celery then sauté for an addition 3 minutes. Add vegetable stock and bring to a boil. Stir in tomato paste, thyme, parsley, Worcestershire sauce, salt and pepper. Reduce heat and simmer for 5 minutes. Remove from heat and let cool.

- In a large bowl mix ground turkey, eggs and bread crumbs. Stir in the vegetable mixture and then form into a loaf, sprinkle with a little salt and place in a non-stick baking pan.

- Bake for 30 minutes. Remove from oven and top with chili sauce. Return to oven and bake for an additional 30 minutes.

chapter 5 - entrées

kevin's mac & cheese by Winemaker Kevin Johansing

Macaroni and cheese is one of Kevin Johansing's favorite foods. As winemaker for Johansing wine and assistant winemaker for Robert Hall, Kevin works up an appetite. His spin on the classic is to skip the bread crumbs, use cottage cheese....and yes beef franks! The crew at Robert Hall loves it when he makes a batch.

Serves 6

16 ounces large macaroni noodles
16 ounces extra sharp cheddar cheese, shredded
8 ounces sour cream
¾ cup 1% milk
16 ounces cottage cheese
3 diced 100% beef franks
Salt and pepper to taste

- Preheat oven to 425F.

- Boil and drain macaroni following package directions. Combine cooked macaroni with all other ingredients in a large bowl. Stir to mix all ingredients.

- Place macaroni and cheese mixture into an oven safe casserole dish and cover with aluminum foil. Bake for 40 minutes and then remove foil. Bake for an additional 10-15 minutes to create a crispy top.

eat this with...

Brady Zinfandel
Johansing Cabernet Sauvignon
Johansing Merlot
Robert Hall Cabernet Sauvignon
Robert Hall Cuvée de Robles

andy's sauerkraut by Andy Heffner

Andy Heffner grew up in Germany, where he enjoyed many traditional sauerkraut and meat dishes. This is his recreation of sauerkraut with pears that his Mother use to make. He recommends serving this with mashed potatoes or parsley potatoes. Feel free to substitute apples or pineapples for the pears.

Serves 8

4 pounds Sauerkraut, drained and rinsed.
2 firm pears, cored and sliced ¼ inch thick
1-2 large onions chopped
1 ½ cups dry white wine
4 tablespoons butter
8 – 10 juniper berries if available
¼ teaspoon allspice ground
Fresh ground pepper
Brown sugar (optional)
Choice of mustards for the sausages when serving.

Meats:

1 Polish Kielbasa
4 smoked pork chops
6 hot Italian sausages
½ pound smoked meat (ham) ¼ inch slices,
Some slices of apple smoked bacon if desired.

- In a large pot melt the butter. Add the sausages and pork chops, and brown (some at a time if they don't all fit in the pan). Remove the meats, add the chopped onions and brown (5 minutes). Add the sliced pears and caramelize, 8 minutes. Add the sauerkraut, white wine and spices, mixing it with scrapings from the meats. Place the meats and sausages on top of the sauerkraut and simmer on low heat for 1-2 hours, stirring occasionally.

- If more sweetness is desired add a sprinkle of brown sugar.

eat this with...
Castoro Cellars Gewurztraminer
Chronic Cellars Riesling
J. Lohr Riesling
Tackitt Fmaily Gewurztraminer

dusi stew and polenta by J. Dusi Wines

This is one of Janell's favorites. Her family is from Northern Italy and a staple in her household growing up was polenta. For generations, polenta and stew has been a family favorite. Apparently the stew recipe has not changed much over the years and Janell remembers sitting around with the family as the stew simmered in a large copper pot on a wood burning stove at her grandparents' home. Janell's mother has been tweaking the recipe to add more flavor. The rosemary, crushed peppers and creamy cheese are all great additions.

Stew

- 2 pounds lean beef, cut in small pieces
- ½ cup flour
- Salt and freshly ground pepper, to taste
- ½ cup olive oil (half for meat, half for veggies)
- 1 large yellow onion, chopped
- 3 cloves of garlic, crushed
- 1 cup diced celery
- 6 carrots, peeled and cut in small pieces
- 1 leek, slice white part and ½ inch of green
- 3 potatoes, peeled and cut in small cubes
- 4 cups beef broth
- 1 cup red wine
- 2 tablespoons Pernod (this is a liqueur)
- Herbs: 2 bay leaves, parsley, thyme, oregano and basil (1 ½ teaspoons of each)
- 2 tablespoons of tomato paste
- 1 cup sweet baby peas

◦ For the Stew: Toss the beef with the ½ cup flour, seasoned with salt and pepper. In a skillet, heat half of the olive oil and brown the beef, a few pieces at a time, then set it aside. In a soup pot, heat the other half of the olive oil. Add the onions, cooking on low for a few minutes. Add the garlic, celery, carrots, leeks and potatoes, stirring to mix up the flavors. Add the beef broth, wine, Pernod, herbs, and tomato paste. Mix all together, then salt and pepper to taste. Cover and simmer on low 2 to 3 hours. It's done when the vegetables are tender. Five minutes before serving, add the sweet baby peas. (for thicker stew, add flour. To thin the stew, add more broth.)

◦ Putting it together: Slice a piece of polenta (see recipe on right hand page) and put it on your plate. Top with a wedge of the soft Tellegio or Tilleme cheese. Cut another slice of polenta, put on top of the cheese. Top the whole thing with stew (Janell recommends pushing on the center of the polenta with a large spoon to create a little bowl for stew).

chapter 5 - entrées

Polenta
¼ pound (1 stick) unsalted butter
¼ cup olive oil
1 tablespoon minced garlic
A dash of crushed red pepper
1 teaspoon minced fresh rosemary leaves
½ teaspoon salt
½ teaspoon coarse black pepper
3 cups chicken stock
2 cups half-and-half
2 cups milk
2 cups polenta
½ cup grated Parmesan cheese
Cheese
4 ounces Tallegio or Tilleme

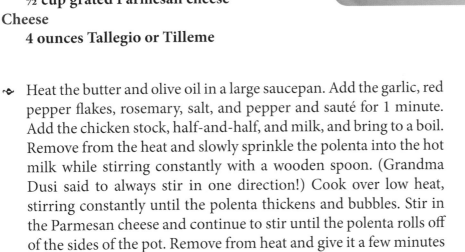

Heat the butter and olive oil in a large saucepan. Add the garlic, red pepper flakes, rosemary, salt, and pepper and sauté for 1 minute. Add the chicken stock, half-and-half, and milk, and bring to a boil. Remove from the heat and slowly sprinkle the polenta into the hot milk while stirring constantly with a wooden spoon. (Grandma Dusi said to always stir in one direction!) Cook over low heat, stirring constantly until the polenta thickens and bubbles. Stir in the Parmesan cheese and continue to stir until the polenta rolls off of the sides of the pot. Remove from heat and give it a few minutes to set up.

eat this with...
J. Dusi Zinfandel

eat this with...
Shale Oak Petite Sirah

paella with kalua pork by Chef Alex Martin, Crush Catering

Serves 8

8 vine-ripened plum tomatoes
Kosher salt
1/4 cup extra-virgin olive oil
3 cups chicken stock
1 small onion, finely chopped
3 cloves garlic, finely chopped
1 1/2 teaspoons smoked paprika
1/4 teaspoon cayenne pepper
1 teaspoon saffron threads
1 large bulb fennel, small dice
1 head of yellow cauliflower, small dice
8 ounces of sweet baby peppers
2 cups dry white wine
2 1/2 cups short-grain paella rice
4 ounces of Sylvetta arugula
8 pounds pork butt
4 tablespoons Hawaiian salt, divided
8 large banana leaves

- **For the Paella:** Preheat the oven to 450 degrees. Core the tomatoes, cut into wedges and place in a medium bowl; season with salt, drizzle with a bit of olive oil and toss. Set aside.

- Heat 1/4 cup olive oil in a 12-inch ovenproof skillet or a paella pan over medium-high heat. Add the onion, garlic, paprika, cayenne and saffron and season with salt. Cook, stirring occasionally, until the onion softens, about 5 minutes. Add the fennel wedges and cook until lightly browned on one side, about 5 minutes. Flip the fennel and add the yellow cauliflower, sweet baby peppers to the skillet; cook until slightly tender, about 4 more minutes. Pour in the wine and simmer until reduced by about one-third. Stir in the rice and 1 3/4 teaspoons salt; add just enough chicken stock to cover the rice completely, 2 1/2 to 3 cups. Increase the heat to high and boil for 2 to 3 minutes. Remove the pan from the heat and arrange the tomatoes on top; drizzle with any tomato juices. Transfer the paella to the oven and bake, undisturbed, for 20 minutes. Turn off the oven but leave the paella inside to continue cooking until the rice is tender, 15 to 20 more minutes. Place Arugula in a medium bowl: season with salt, drizzle with a bit of olive oil and toss. Garnish arugula on top of Paella.

- **For the Kalua Pork:** After scoring pork on all sides with 1/4-inch deep slits about 1-inch apart, rub with 3 tablespoons salt. Wrap the pork completely in banana leaves, tie with string, and wrap in foil. Place meat in a shallow roasting pan with 2 cups of water and roast for 8 hours at 250 degrees F. Shred the cooked pork and top paella with pork.

tenderloin of pork with apricots by Tablas Creek Vineyard

This recipe is a Haas family favorite for the winter months. The fruit of the apricots and the natural earthiness of the pork enhances the intense fruit and spicy, smoky flavors of the Esprit.

Serves 6

3 pounds pork tenderloin, cut into 1 inch cubes
1 pound dried apricot halves
1 cup seedless raisins
2 cups dry red wine
1/2 cup red wine vinegar
3 tablespoons chopped fresh parsley
3 tablespoons chopped fresh mint
1 teaspoon ground cumin

1 teaspoon freshly ground black pepper
1 tablespoon dried thyme
salt, to taste
4 tablespoons olive oil
4 shallots, peeled and minced
2 cups chicken stock
2 bay leaves
3 tablespoons honey

- In a large bowl, combine pork, apricots, raisins, 1 1/2 cups wine, vinegar, parsley, mint, cumin, pepper, thyme, and salt to taste. Cover and marinate, refrigerated, for 4 hours. Stir occasionally.

- Remove pork and fruit from marinade, reserving marinade. Place fruit in a small bowl. Pat pork dry with paper towel.

- Heat olive oil in large skillet and saute meat, a few pieces at a time, until well browned. With a slotted spoon, transfer pork to a deep casserole.

- Drain oil from skillet, add shallots, and saute over medium heat for 5 minutes. Add reserved marinade and bring to a boil, scraping up any browned bits remaining in the skillet. Cook for several minutes, until slightly reduced, and add to the casserole.

- Stir in apricots, raisins, remaining 1/2 cup of wine, chicken stock, bay leaves and honey; mix well. Set over medium heat, bring to a boil, cover, and set on the middle rack of the oven, preheated to 375F. Bake for 2 hours, or until meat is tender and sauce rich and thick.

- Serve over rice or couscous.

eat this with...
Tablas Creek Esprit de Beaucastel

pork kebabs by Julie Simon, Thomas Hill Organics

These middle eastern kebabs are ideal served with tabbouleh salad and a spicy harissa.

Serves 4
- **2 pounds of boneless country style pork ribs**
- **2 tablespoons of rosemary, chopped**
- **4 garlic cloves, crushed**
- **2 lemons, zest and juice**
- **4 oranges, zest and juice**
- **6 tablespoons of honey**
- **1 teaspoon of chili flakes**
- **1 tablespoon fennel seeds**
- **1 tablespoon of cracked pepper**
- **Kosher salt**

eat this with...
J. Dusi Zinfandel
Red Soles Estate Zinfandel
Pear Valley Zinfandel
Ranchita Canyon Zinfandel
Robert Hall Zinfandel

- Cut pork nto 1 1/4 inch cubes.

- Lay paper towels on a flat surface where you will lay the meat and more paper towels so the pork is "dry". Then place the pork into a bowl and add all the other ingredients (minus salt). Cover tightly and refrigerate for about 2 and up to 4 hours.

- Thread meat onto skewer, season with salt. Place the reserved marinade into a little saucepan and bring to a boil.

- On a medium high heat and well-seasoned grill, cook the skewers, without moving them around too much to optimize caramelization. Brush them regularly with the marinade for about 10 minutes.

- Serve with spicy harissa.

chapter 5 - entrées

teriyaki flank steak by Ranchita Canyon Vineyard

Teresa Hinrichs adds the flavors of Asia to her flank steak. This teriyaki recipes uses just a few flavorful ingredients -- give yourself some time to allow the marinade to tenderize the meat.

Serves 4-6
> 2 pounds flank steak
> 1/2 cup low-sodium soy sauce
> 1/2 cup mirin
> ½ cup rice vinegar
> 3 tablespoons sugar

- Prepare the flank steak by scoring the meat on both sides, in a crisscross pattern to allow the marinade to absorb into the meat. In a small bowl combine the low-sodium soy sauce, mirin, rice vinegar, and sugar. Place the steak and marinade in a zip lock bag and marinate for 4-24 hours. Reserve a small portion of the marinade for basting the meat as it cooks.

- Grill the steak for about 4 minutes until seared, flip it over and grill for another 4 minutes for medium (for a 1/2 inch thick steak.) Baste with reserved marinade as it cooks. Cut into thin, diagonal across the grain slices.

eat this with...
Ranchita Canyon Cabernet Franc

crown roast by Lisa Pretty

There is something about a crown roast that makes it seem so elegant and special – your guest will think they are royalty when the crown is presented.

Yield

8 pound lamb (or pork) crown roast
2 tablespoons fresh chopped rosemary
1 teaspoon dried thyme
2 teaspoons sea salt
1 cup dry white wine
¼ cup olive oil
1 cup water

Stuffing

½ stick butter
2 medium onions, chopped
4 stalks celery, chopped
2 teaspoons dried thyme
1 teaspoon dried sage
Salt & pepper to taste
1 French baguette, cubed

- Pre heat oven to 400F.

- In a medium frying pan melt the butter and sauté the onions and celery. Stir in the thyme, sage, salt and pepper. Continue to sauté until the onions are soft then toss with bread in a large bowl.

- Place roast in a large roasting pan, bone side up, with the crown forming a perfect circle. Sprinkle the roast with rosemary, thyme and salt then fill the center of the crown with stuffing. Place any remaining stuffing in a greased baking dish. Pour wine and water around the roast in the base of the pan.

- Roast for 30 minutes. Pour juice from the bottom of the pan over the roast and the top of stuffing. Cover the stuffing and the bone tips with foil. Reduce heat to 350F and place pan back in the oven to continue roasting. Place pan with extra stuffing in the oven approximately 30 minutes prior to the roast being done. The roast will take approximately 20 minutes per pound.

- When the roast reaches 155F remove from the oven and let it rest for 10 minutes prior to serving.

eat this with...

Brady Petite Sirah
Kukkula in the red
LVX Crimson Jewel
Pear Valley Distraction
Penman Springs Petite Syrah
Robert Hall Pape de Robles

pork puttanesca by Chef Thomas Drahos, Avant-Garde Catering

Puttanesca sauce was created by the "ladies" in the red light district. The wonderful aroma brought the hungry men to the door. Chef Thomas likely had a different audience in mind when he created his recipe!

Spicy tomato sauce

- 1 tablespoon chili flakes
- 1 tablespoon garlic, finely chopped
- 2 cans crushed tomatoes
- 1 bunch of basil
- 1 medium white onion, diced
- 1 tablespoon dried oregano
- 1 tablespoon olive oil

- Preheat a medium sauce pot over high heat, and add oil followed by everything except the tomatoes. Cook until the onions have taken on a golden color. Add the tomatoes and reduce to low heat, simmer for thirty minutes. Blend on high speed in a blender to create a nice consistency. Reserve for later use.

Oven roasted Pork loin

- 3 pounds of pork loin
- Salt and pepper
- 3 tablespoons olive oil

- Preheat the oven to 400 degrees. Heat a large sauté pan over high heat, add the oil. Season pork loin liberally and sear until golden brown on all sides of the loin. Place in oven and roast until internal temperature reaches 150 degrees remove and rest for five minutes before slicing.

- To plate, place a large spoonful of spicy tomato sauce in the middle of a plate next put three shingled slices about ¼ inch thick of pork loin on top of the sauce. Next put one spoon full of dehydrated tapenade on the pork loin in the middle garnish with 5 nice leaves of parsley.

Dehydrated tapenade

- 1 can green olive
- 1 can kalamata olives
- 1 jar cappers

- Preheat your dehydrator to 145 degrees. Rinse all brine off olives and capers and place in a colander to drain off the water then dry them using paper towels. Mix all ingredients in a bowl evenly. Spread mixture over the dehydrator trays and dehydrate for 10 hours or until dry. Reserve in a air tight container.

eat this with...

Eberle Sangiovese
Niner Sangiovese
Le Vigne Sangiovese
Opolo Sangiovese
Pear Valley Aglianico
Ranchita Canyon Sangiovese

chapter 5 - entrées

stuffed rolled pork roast by Lisa Pretty

This pork roast is pretty on the plate and pairs well with a wide range of wines

Serves 8
>   **4-5 pound pork roast**
>   **Sea salt, to taste**

Sauce
½ cup Port
1 pint fresh figs, chopped
4 tablespoons pomegranate molasses
Stuffing
3 ounces pancetta, chopped
1 onion, chopped
2 cloves garlic, minced
1 teaspoon dried thyme

- Place port and figs in a small sauce pan and bring to a boil. Stir in pomegranate molasses and reduce heat to simmer. Continue to simmer until sauce thickens (approximately 15 minutes). Drain sauce through a sieve to remove and skin and seeds. Set aside as you prepare the other components.

- Preheat oven to 400F.

- In a medium frying pan sauté the pancetta for 3 minutes. Add the onions, garlic and thyme and continue to sauté. When the onions are soft, remove from heat and stir in the bread crumbs and dried fruit.

- Using a sharp knife, cut the pork roast approximately 1 inch thick in a spiral so that when you are finished the roast is a large rectangle. Pour half of the sauce over the pork, then layer with stuffing 1.5 inches from the edges. Roll the pork like a jelly roll and tie with kitchen string. Place fat side up in a roasting pan and sprinkle with a little sea salt.

- Roast pork at 400F for 15 minutes then reduce heat to 350F. Roast for an additional 30-45 minutes (use a meat thermometer to check that the pork is 160F). Remove from the oven and let rest for 10 minutes prior to removing string and slicing.

- Serve topped with the reserved sauce.

eat this with...

Caliza Azimuth
Clavo Collusion
Kukkula in the red
Parrish Family Vineyard Silken
Pear Valley Inspiration
Penman Springs Meritage
Pretty-Smith Palette de Rouge
Robert Hall Meritage

mutton curry by Neeta Mittal, LXV Wines

India is a culture you can taste! This finger licking, authentic, fragrant, flavorful curry is made with tender pieces of mutton (meat of adult sheep). You could substitute goat meat.

Serves 6
- 1 pound mutton (cut into 1 inch pieces)
- 1 large onion, finely chopped
- 2 medium tomatoes, finely chopped
- 2 tablespoons vegetable oil

Marinade:
- 1/2 teaspoon turmeric powder
- 3 garlic cloves
- 1 inch ginger
- 1 bunch coriander leaves
- 1 cup yogurt
- 1/2 teaspoon garam masala
- 2 teaspoons salt

Mutton Masala
- 2 teaspoon coriander seeds
- 1 teaspoon cumin seeds
- 3 green cardamom
- 4 dry red chilies
- 2 teaspoon fried onions
- 2 teaspoon dry grated coconut
- 1 teaspoon sesame seeds
- 1/2 teaspoon black pepper
- 3-4 cloves
- 1 inch cinnamon stick
- 1 black cardamom
- 1 star anise

- Grind all mutton masala ingredients together. Set aside.

- Mix the marinade ingredients in a blender and apply them to the mutton. Set aside for at least 3 hours. Then cook the mutton in a pressure cooker. Allow 3 whistles, then turn off. Do not open the cooker immediately, wait for 20 minutes.

- Meanwhile, fry the onions in vegetable oil until golden brown and translucent. Add the tomatoes and fry until the oil leaves the mixture. Add the cooked meat and 5 teaspoons of mutton masala. Reduce the juices of the mutton in the open cooker, until a smooth gravy forms. Garnish with chopped coriander leaves.

Note: There is really no substitute for a pressure cooker, if you want the flavors to penetrate the soft meat. A pan with a very heavy lid may work.

eat this with...
LXV Rising Tempo

game meat pie by Steve Mayer/Chris Pedone wildgamewine.com

This hearty dish is a meal in itself. You can vary the ingredients tremendously and have a truly unique pie. Any kind of game meat will work wonderfully! You can use any variety of cheese or any type of potatoes you desire. If you don't want to use the pastry crust it will be a great shepherd's pie with just the potatoes as a crust. Feel free to experiment with different meats, cheeses, potatoes and vegetables. Get creative! I don't think you can make a bad pie. It is a pretty forgiving recipe.

Serves 4-6

- 1 puff pastry sheet
- 1 medium onion chopped (1 cup)
- 1 tablespoon olive oil
- 1 tablespoon butter
- 1 pound ground game meat
- 1 teaspoon kosher salt
- 1 teaspoon black pepper
- ½ teaspoon Italian seasoning
- 1 ½ teaspoon Worcestershire sauce
- 1/2 pound mixed frozen vegetables
- 1 ten ounce can cream of mushroom soup
- ½ pound of grated sharp cheddar cheese
- 1 egg

Garlic Mashed Potatoes

- 1 head of garlic
- 3 medium russet potatoes
- ¾ cup heavy cream or milk
- ¼ stick butter
- ½ teaspoon kosher salt
- ½ teaspoon black pepper
- ¼ cup chopped parsley
- Paprika

chapter 5 - entrées

- For Potatoes: Roast the garlic .Place head of garlic on a sheet of foil. Drizzle a little olive oil over it, and wrap in the foil. Roast in the oven for 45 minutes at 375 degrees F.

- Remove one frozen puff pastry shell from the package, let thaw on the counter and unfold.

- Bring a large pot of salted water to a boil. Wash, (peeled or not based on your preference), and cut the potatoes into 1" cubes. Boil the potatoes about 20 minutes until fork tender. Drain the water off, and squeeze 6-10 cloves of the roasted garlic onto the potatoes. Add the cream, butter, salt and pepper, and mash until well blended. Add chopped parsley and set aside.

- For Rest of Pie: In a large frying pan add the butter and olive oil and warm up over medium heat. Saute the chopped onion in this mixture about 5 minutes until the onion is translucent. Add the game meat, salt, pepper, Italian seasoning, and Worcestershire sauce and simmer until cooked (about 5 minutes). Stir in the can of cream of mushroom soup, the frozen vegetables, and remove from heat.

- Grease a deep 9" casserole dish and add meat mixture to it. Layer the grated cheese over the meat, and spoon the potatoes over the cheese. Sprinkle the potatoes with paprika and lay the pastry crust over the top. Conform the crust to the edges of the dish and seal the pie in. Crimp the excess if you want.

- Prepare an egg wash by beating an egg with one tablespoon of water. Brush this mixture over the top of the crust. Bake the pie in the middle of a pre-heated 400 degree F oven for 15 – 20 minutes or until golden brown. Remove from the oven and let sit for 5 -10 minutes.

- Serve with a dressed mixed green salad.

eat this with...

Clavo Syrah
Graveyard Reserve Syrah
Kukkula i.p.o.
Red Soles Tempranillo
Ranchita Canyon Cabernet Franc

chapter 5 - entrées

CHEF PROFILE: *Chef Alexander Martin*

Chef Alex started Crush Catering in October 2011. Alex's passion for food started in High School where he had the chance to attend the Paso Robles Culinary Academy; where he worked with C.E.C Phillip Riccomini. That inspired him to attend the C.S.C.A Le Cordon Bleu in Pasadena, California. He also gained valuable experience while working for Wolfgang Puck Catering Co. and at Traxx Restaurant located at the Historic Union Station in Downtown L.A. After culinary school Alex returned home to the central coast where he assisted as Sous Chef in the implementation of opening Matthew's at the Airport alongside C.E.C. Matthew Riley. After 2 years at Matthew's, Alex was presented with the opportunity to open Panolivo Restaurant in San Luis Obispo as Executive Chef. Alex always had an eye for baking and pastries, but never dove deep into it, but when working at Artisan Restaurant with Chef Chris Kobayashi, the challenge arose. Alex wanted to be a well rounded chef; and becoming Pastry Chef at Artisan was an amazing opportunity. Alex later went on to perfect his skills at Justin Vineyards & Winery as Sous Chef. Alex is a three time Pinot and Paella Cook-off winner and competed in the 2009 Confrerie de la Chaine des Rotisseurs Regional Young Chef Competition where he placed second. Alex won the 2011, 2012 Olive Festival Head to Head Cook-off in a iron chef style competition. 1st place in the 2012 Wellness Kitchen Top Chef Cook off featuring gluten free and vegan dishes showed Alex's diversity as a chef. Just recently Alex also won first place in the 2013 CWA Creston Burger Cook-Off. Inspiration is brought to him every day by local farmers, winemakers, and guest chefs from around the world.

grilled lamb chops by Ian McPhee, McPhee's Grill

Ian McPhee recommends serving these grilled Lamb Chops with roasted grapes & zinfandel sauce along side your favorite mashed potates with a little fresh goat cheese mixed in.

Serves 4

8 loin lamb chops
2 teaspoon minced mint
1 teaspoon minced rosemary
¼ cup olive oil
1 tablespoon olive oil
1pound red grapes on stem
½ teaspoon honey
½ teaspoon rough chopped mint
¼ teaspoon rosemary leaves
½ cup zinfandel wine
2 tablespoons chilled butter

- Mix rosemary, mint & olive oil together. Spread over lamb chops marinate for one hour. When ready, simply grill the chops till your favorite doneness.

- Break red grapes into small portions (still attached to stems). In a wide fry pan heat olive oil on medium heat, add grapes, let them cook, tossing often. When they start to soften add honey, mint, rosemary and wine. Let wine reduce till slightly syrupy. Turn off heat and add chilled butter tossing to coat grapes. Place grape stems next to lamb and pour sauce over the lamb.

eat this with...
Clavo Zinfandel
J. Dusi Zinfandel
Opolo Zinfandel
Pear valley Zinfandel
Robert Hall Syrah
Robert Hall Zinfandel
Shale Oak Zinfandel

lamb orecchiette by Lisa Pretty

Whenever I make this recipe for my friends they lick the bowl clean. The ground lamb is the star of this dish -- it just isn't the same with other ground meats.

Serves 4
1 tablespoon olive oil
1 small yellow onion, finely chopped
1 pound ground lamb
1 tablespoon finely chopped fresh rosemary
28-ounce can of diced tomatoes
2 tablespoons tomato paste
1 teaspoon cayenne pepper
Salt and pepper, to taste
1 cup frozen peas
4 cups cooked orecchiette
½ cup shredded Italian cheese

- Heat olive oil in a large frying pan. Sauté onions for 3-5 minutes over medium heat. Add the ground lamb to the pan and cook until brown, continually stirring. Stir in rosemary, tomatoes, tomato paste and salt and pepper. Bring to a boil and then reduce heat to simmer. Allow sauce to simmer for 1 hour.

- While the sauce is simmering cook orecchiette following package directions.

- Add peas to the sauce and simmer for an additional 45 minutes. Stir in hot pasta. Serve in bowls garnished with the shredded cheese.

leg of lamb by Chef Charles D. Paladin Wayne

Roasted leg of lamb Seasoned with Garlic, Mustard, Mint and Rosemary pairs well with a wide range of Paso red wine. Several local farms offer quality lambs for sale in the Spring.

Serves 10

1 6-pound boneless leg of lamb (netted)
¼ cup Dijon mustard
4 sprigs rosemary, picked and chopped fine
4 sprigs mint, picked and chopped fine
20 cloves of garlic, sliced in half
Salt & pepper, to taste

eat this with...
Clavo Compadre
Broken Earth Merlot
Pear Valley Inspiration
Pretty-Smith Palette de Rouge
Shale Oak Petit Verdot

- Preheat oven to 400F.

- Take the lamb leg out of the net and unfold in a roasting pan.

- Combine the chopped mint and the rosemary with the mustard and half the garlic. Salt and pepper the inside and outside of the lamb. Rub the inside of the roast with the mustard mixture and fold together again and put the net back on.

- Using a paring knife, make 20 punctures into the leg through the net and insert a half clove of garlic. Place into a preheated oven 400F. Cook for 30 minutes then reduce the heat to 325F and cook for 2 hours. Let rest out of the oven for 20 minutes slice and serve.

chapter 5 - entrées

braised lamb shank by Il Cortile Ristorante

A bone-in lamb shank is a heavenly dish. I have a couple of friends who order this dish every time they dine at Il Cortile.

Serves 4

    3 tablespoons of olive oil
    2 tablespoons thyme
    I ½ tablespoons rosemary
    3-4 bay leaves
    1 cinnamon stick
    2 .5 cups of red wine
    2 cups of beef stock
    Flour for dusting
    4 12-ounce lamb shanks, bone in

- Heat the oven to 400F.

- Sprinkle salt and pepper to taste on the lamb shanks. Dust the shanks with the flour. Cook the wine for 2 -3 minutes to burn off all the alcohol. In a large frying pan, heat the oil. Brown the shanks on all sides and set aside in a braising pan. Reserve the oil and any juices left from the shanks. Add the wine to deglaze the pan. Add the thyme, rosemary. Cook for 2- 3 minutes. Add the bay leaves and cinnamon stick. Cook for 2 -3 minutes. Add the beef stock and simmer for 2-3 minutes.

- Pour the mixture over the lamb shanks and cover very well. Cook for 3 hours or until the meat is falling off the bone.

- Plate the lamb shanks on warm plates. Put the juices from the pan into a sauté pan and cook the juices for about 3 minutes. Pour over the lamb shanks and serve.

eat this with...
Broken Earth Tempranillo
J. Lohr Hilltop Cabernet Sauvignon
Pear Valley Cabernet Franc
Robert Hall Pape de Robles

chapter 5 - entrées

grilled strip loin by Will Torres, The Restaurant at JUSTIN

Grilled Charter Oak Strip Loin with Charred Onion-Tomatillo Relish and Corn Espuma

eat this with...
JUSTIN ISOSCELES

For Steak:
- 4 Charter Oak strip loin (8-10 ounces each)
- Maldon sea salt
- Fresh black pepper
- 4 tablespoons extra virgin olive oil

For Charred Onion-Tomatillo Relish
- 1/2 pound tomatillos cut in ½" slices
- 2 small red onions cut in ½" slices
- 1 jalapeno, halved and seeded
- 1/4 cup extra virgin olive oil
- 1 Garlic Clove, sliced thin
- Salt
- 3 tablespoons cilantro, chopped fine
- 3 tablespoons parsley, chopped fine
- 1 tablespoon fresh lime juice
- 1 tablespoon apple cider vinegar
- 1 tablespoon sugar

Sweet Corn Espuma
- 4 ounces sweet corn
- 8 ounces milk (chef likes Straus)
- 8 ounces cream (chef likes Straus)
- Maldon sea salt
- Fresh black pepper
- Sugar
- 3 gelatin sheets, bloomed in cold water
- 1 iSi Gourmet Whipper
- 2 iSi N20 charges

- For Steak: Pre-Heat gas or charcoal grill to med-high heat. Rub the steaks with olive oil and sprinkle with salt and pepper. Grill the steak for 4 to 6 minutes on one side, and then flip and continue to cook until medium-rare, 3 to 4 more minutes. Let rest, and then slice.

- For Relish: In a large bowl, toss the tomatillos, onion, and jalapeno in extra virgin olive oil. Add sliced garlic. Season with salt and refrigerate for 30 minutes. Grill the tomatillos until charred on one side, about 3 minutes, and grill the onion and jalapeno, turning once, until crisp-tender and slightly charred, about 8 minutes. Finely chop the vegetables and transfer to a bowl. Stir in cilantro, parsley, lime juice, vinegar, and sugar. Adjust seasoning with salt and pepper.

- For Sweet Corn Espuma: Warm the milk, cream and corn. Turn off heat and steep for 20 min. Blend together on high for 5 min. Strain and adjust seasoning with salt pepper and sugar. Strain and whisk in gelatin. Place in iSi gourmet whipper and charge with 2 N2O charges. Keep warm or chill.

CHEF PROFILE: Chef Will Torres

Chef Will developed a passion and love for food and cooking at a very young age while watching his Grandfather and Mother cook in the kitchen. This passion was the driving force in his attending the California School of Culinary Arts in Pasadena, CA. where he graduated with top honors in 2003. While attending C.S.C.A., he gained valuable experience in the kitchen working on events for Spago Catering, Patina, The Playboy Mansion, and Aubergine Restaurant in Newport Beach. Will began his culinary career at the elite West Hollywood hot spot KOI for a year working his way through the different stations in the kitchen and taking on a leadership role. In 2005, Will accepted the role of Sous Chef at JUSTIN where he was able to show us his skill and instinct for the culinary arts.

Will accepted the position as the Executive Chef of JUSTIN Vineyards & Winery in 2009 and could not be more excited with the new kitchen, restaurant and menu.

tri tip with salsa by Lisa Pretty

Tri tip barbecues are a Paso Robles favorite. I first discovered Tri Tip when I moved to the Central Coast. I have to confess to not being a huge fan until I tried Gary Eberle's. This is my take on his Tri Tip and salsa.

Serves 8
 1 Tri Tip roast
 Salt & Pepper to taste

Marinade
 ½ cup rosemary infused
 white wine vinegar
 ¼ cup olive oil
 2 cloves garlic, crushed

Salsa
 ½ cup chopped grape tomatoes
 3 tomatillos, chopped
 ¼ cup chopped cilantro
 3 cloves garlic, chopped
 3 green onions, chopped
 ¼ teaspoon cumin
 Salt and pepper, to taste

eat this with...
Broken Earth Quadrant Platinum
Eberle Cabernet Sauvignon
Penman Springs Merlot
Robert Hall Merlot

- Combine marinade ingredients. Place roast in a large zip lock bag and pour marinade over top. Remove air from bag, seal and place in refrigerator to marinate for at least 4 hours to overnight.

- Remove roast from bag and discard marinade. Season with salt and pepper then place on sear section of a gas grill. Turn roast frequently to sear on all sides. Once roast has a nice sear move to medium-low heat on the grill and cook approximately 25 minutes longer, turning occasionally. Remove from grill and allow to rest for 5-10 minutes.

- While meat rests, combine salsa ingredients. Slice roast thin, across the grain. Serve topped with salsa or on the side.

chapter 5 - entrées

skirt steak roule by Chef Andre, Paso Terra Seafood

Skirt Steak Roule with Wild Mushroom and Wine Reduction sauce is a perfect winter entrée.

Serves 1
- **8 ounce skirt steak**
- **4 mushrooms, sliced**
- **1 clove garlic minced**
- **1 tablespoon tomato paste**
- **1 tablespoon brandy**
- **1 tablespoon butter**
- **2 oounces shallots, minced**
- **½ bottle red wine**

- Pound steak into long strip and roll tightly. Place roll standing up in a kitchen town and wrap tightly. Pound roll into a flat round, looking like filet. Sauté steak in canola oil and remove.

- Add mushroom to the pan and cook until colored. Add shallots, garlic and cook until transparent. Add tomato paste and cook until tomato paste gives off strong aroma. Add wine and cook until sauce it becomes syrupy. Finish with brandy and butter.

- Place steak on plate and top with sauce. Serve with polenta or potatoes and seaonal vegetables.

eat this with...
Brady Petite Sirah
Clavo Malbec
Graveyard Petite Sirah
Kukkula in the red
Pear Valley Distraction

pan roasted ribeye steak by Chef Natalie Dorris

This French bistro inspired entrée was a Colby Jack favorite. Chef Natalie loves how versatile the components of this dish are. The steak can be served whole with scalloped potatoes and asparagus or sliced, served on toasted French bread and topped with the butter and onions for an impressive appetizer. While the caramelized onions and compound butter would be great stuffed in a chicken breast or topping a hearty beef stew.

Serves 4

eat this with...

Caliza Syrah
J. Dusi Zinfandel
JUSTIN Cabernet Sauvignon
Pear Valley Cabernet Sauvignon
Pomar Junction Merlot
Robert Hall Merlot
Ranchita Canyon Malbec
Shale Oak Petite Sirah

For Butter
4 ounces butter (1 stick), very soft
4 ounces blue cheese crumbles
1 tablespoon freshly chopped parsley
1 teaspoon minced garlic
1 teaspoon minced shallot
Salt and pepper

For Onions
1 pound onions, thinly sliced
1 tablespoon butter
1 tablespoon olive oil
1 tablespoon sugar

For Steak
4 10-ounce Ribeye prime (about 1 1/4 to 1 1/2 inches thick)
2 teaspoons extra-virgin olive oil, divided
1 teaspoon minced fresh thyme
Coarse kosher salt and course ground pepper

French Bread

- For compound butter: In a medium bowl, beat the butter, blue cheese, parsley, garlic, shallot, and salt and pepper until blended. Place butter mixture in the center of a large piece of plastic wrap. Roll into a sausage shape. Refrigerate for up to 3 days, or freeze for up to 2 weeks.

- For onions: Heat a skillet on med-low heat. Add oil and butter. Cook the onions until clear and soft (with no color on them). This will take a few minutes. Once soft (but not brown) turn heat up to medium and add sugar. Stir constantly until onions are dark caramel color and very soft (20-30 minutes total). **using a non-stick pan can inhibit the browning process, increasing the cooking time.

- For steak: Rub steak with 1 teaspoon oil; sprinkle both sides with thyme, then coarse salt and 1/4 teaspoon black pepper. Let steak stand at room temperature 30 minutes. Heat medium sized skillet over medium-high heat. Add steak; cook to desired doneness, 3 to 4 minutes per side for medium-rare. If a more done steak is desired, put pan in 400 degree oven, checking at 2 minute intervals for desired doneness. Let rest on plate for a couple minutes before serving.

- To plate: Place steak on plate. Slice a piece of butter off log and put on-top of steak. Put about a couple of ounces of onions on top. Garnish with fresh thyme.

- As an appetizer: Slice French bread thinly on a diagonal, brush with olive oil and season with salt and pepper, heat in oven until lightly toasted. Spread blue butter on toast. Top with thin slice of steak, top steak with some caramelize onions, garnish with chopped thyme or parsley.

braised shortribs by Tablas Creek Vineyard

Braised sortribs with black olives is wonderfully comforting on a winter night. The flaming brandy, although not absolutely essential, burns up the excess fat and makes quite a difference to the flavor of the finished sauce.

Serves 6

5 poounds bone-in short ribs, trimmed of excess fat
4 tablespoons brandy
8 ounces red wine
6-8 ounces chicken stock or water
1 tablespoon butter
1 tablespoon olive oil

6 ounces pitted black olives, rinsed
Bouquet of thyme, parsley and bay leaf
Strip of orange peel
2 crushed garlic cloves
Salt and pepper to taste

- Preheat oven to 300F.

- In large pot on medium-high, brown the meat in the olive oil and butter, in batches. Return all meat to pan, and arrange ribs in single layer.

- Warm brandy in a soup ladle, pour it over the meat, carefully set a light to it, and shake the pan until flames go out. Add the red wine and enough stock to come halfway up the sides of the ribs. Let it bubble quickly for about 30 seconds.

- Lightly season with salt and pepper, add the bouquet, orange peel and garlic. Cover pot with a layer of foil and the lid. Cook in oven for 2 to 2 1/2 hours, until meat is fork-tender. Check periodically to make sure liquid is simmering and not drying up.

- Ten minutes before serving, remove bouquet and add olives. Stir to combine.

- Serve with egg noodles or rice.

eat this with...
Tablas Creek Côtes de Tablas
Tablas Creek Esprit de Tablas
Tablas Creek Tannat

eat this with...
Broken Earth Petit Verdot
Caliza Syrah
Halter Ranch Syrah
Locatelli Malbec
Pear Valley Distraction
Penman Springs Meritage
Ranchita Canyon Petite Sirah
Robert Hall Pape de Robles
Steinbeck The Crash

braised short ribs with polenta by Chef Ryan Swarthout

Braised Short Ribs with Creamy Polenta, Red Wine Braised Carrots and Braising Sauce Reduction

Short Ribs:
- 4 pounds short ribs
- Salt and pepper
- 4 tablespoon olive oil
- 1 onion, quartered
- 2 celery stalks, chopped
- 5 carrots, peeled and cut into 1 inch
- 4 garlic gloves, crushed
- 1 bay leaf
- 2 cups red wine
- 5-6 cups beef stock

Creamy Polenta:
- 4 cups water
- 4 cups milk
- 3 tablespoon butter
- 2 teaspoon salt
- 2 cups polenta
- ½ cup crème fraiche
- 1/3 cup Parmesan cheese, grated
- 1 tablespoon rosemary, chopped
- 1 teaspoon thyme, chopped
- 1 teaspoon oregano, chopped

- Short Ribs: Heat the oil in an oven safe pot over high heat. Season the short ribs with salt and pepper. Carefully place into the heated pan and brown on all sides. Remove and reserve. Add all the vegetable and sauté. Add the short ribs back into the pan and deglaze with the red wine. Add the bay leaf and beef stock. Bring to a boil. Cover and place in a preheated 375 degree oven and cook for 3-3 ½ hours. Once the beef is cooked remove from braising liquid. Reserve the braised carrots, garlic and 4 cups of braising liquid. Defat the braising liquid by skimming the top. Place in a small sauce pot and reduce by ¾ or until thick.

- Polenta: In a large sauce pan bring the water, milk and butter to a boil. Add salt and whisk in the polenta. Whisk consistently for 3-4 minutes to prevent lumps. Simmer for 45 minutes partially covered stirring every 10 minutes until polenta is thick, smooth and creamy. Add crème fraiche, Parmesan and chopped herbs. Check season and adjust consistency by adding milk or water to polenta.

- Assembly: Spoon 1- 1 ½ cups of polenta into a shallow bowl. Place the braised short ribs on top of the polenta and the carrots and garlic around the edge of the polenta. Pour a generous amount of sauce over beef and around. Garnish with rosemary sprig.

chapter 6 - desserts

grilled peaches by Lisa Pretty

When peaches are in season this is the perfect dessert to serve when you do not want to use an oven, stove or spend much time prepping. Yogurt and blueberries offer a nice complement to the basil and peaches.

Serves 4

- 2 fresh peaches – ripe but still firm
- 2 tablespoons of olive oil
- ¼ cup orange muscat (or Triple Sec Orange Liqueur)
- 2 tablespoons chopped fresh basil
- 2 tablespoons Greek yogurt (optional)
- ¼ cup fresh blueberries

- Wash peaches and cut in half. Remove pit and place in a shallow bowl.

- Mix together the olive oil, wine and basil. Pour mixture over the peaches and cover. Allow the peaches to marinate for 15-30 minutes, spooning liquid over the peaches a couple of times.

- Heat grill to medium. Place peaches cut side down and grill for approximately 3 minutes. The peaches should just start to show grill marks but not become too soft.

- Serve as is or top with Greek yogurt and blueberries.

eat this with...
Broken Earth White Star
Caliza Viognier
LXV Summer Satine
Pear Valley Orange Muscat
Robert Hall Orange Muscat

baked plums by Chef Thomas Drahos, Avant-Garde Catering

Baked plums, honey glazed puffed rice, and chocolate gel with a touch of mint and whipped cream. This dessert will wow your guests with the burst of flavor and beautiful presentation.

Serves 4

- 4 plums (cut in half and pitted)
- 1 tablespoon cinnamon
- 2 tablespoons sugar
- 3 cups rice (cooked)
- 5 cups of frying oil
- 1 cup of local honey
- 2 cups of simple syrup
- 2 ounces organic fair trade chocolate 72%
- 8 grams powder agar
- Mint sprigs for garnish (optional
- Whipped cream for garnish (optional)

eat this with...
LXV Summer Satine
Pear Valley Belle Fin
Pomar Junction Amber Moonlight

- **Baked Plums:** Preheat the oven to 300 degrees. On a sheet pan lined with parchment paper lay plums cut side up and sprinkle with cinnamon and sugar. Bake for ten minutes or until tender. Reserve

- **Honey glazed puffed Rice:** Place cooked rice on a sheet pan spread out evenly and dry for twenty four hours, uncovered (this moves faster if you place the pan on top of a warm place). Once rice is dry heat you oil to a smoking 500 degrees. Carefully place rice in the oil a little at a time about a cup or so. Remove once golden. Once all rice is puffed add the honey and mix to incorporate.

- **Chocolate gel:** Heat simple syrup and chocolate until boiling in a small sauce pot. Next add agar and drop heat to a simmer. Simmer for 8 minutes remove from heat and pour through a fine mesh strainer into a shallow container. Let chill until completely solid. Cut gel into cubes and blend on high speed until mixture is smooth and silky (adding water to help with blending if needed).

- **To plate:** Place one baked plum in the center of a white plate, sprinkle plums with more sugar and torch to bruleé. Put a mound of honey glazed puffed rice on top and then put on dot of chocolate gel down, using a spoon drag to create a line through the gel. Garnish with mint sprigs and whipped cream.

blackberry clafoutis by Lisa Pretty

Clafoutis, a traditional French dish, is a baked custard-like dessert typically made with cherries and dusted with powdered sugar. Like many popular desserts, over the years people tend to tweak the recipe and there are many variations that take a twist on the classic. This recipe uses blackberries instead of cherries and much less sugar than traditional recipes. An advantage of making a dessert that is not overly sweet is that it pairs well with dry wines as well as dessert wines.

Serves 8

1 tablespoon butter, at room temperature

1 ½ cups blackberries

¼ cup granulated sugar

3 eggs

6 tablespoons all purpose flour

1 cup whipping cream

½ cup whole milk

2 teaspoons vanilla extract

Zest of one lemon

¼ teaspoon salt

¼ cup powdered sugar

eat this with...

Brady Petite Sirah

Pear Valley Grenache

Pomar Junction Train Wreck

Pretty-Smith Cabernet Sauvignon

Steinbeck Zinfandel

Vista Del Rey Barbera

- ❧ Preheat the oven to 375F.

- ❧ Butter a 10-inch round, deep-dish pie dish and arrange blackberries in the dish.

- ❧ Beat the eggs and sugar on high speed using an electric mixer until light and fluffy. On low speed, mix in the flour, cream, milk, vanilla, lemon zest, and salt. Set aside for 10 minutes.

- ❧ Pour the batter over the berries and bake until the top is golden brown and the custard is firm, 35 to 40 minutes.

- ❧ Sprinkle with powdered sugar and serve lukewarm.

chapter 6 - desserts

peach cobbler by Chef Julie Simon, Thomas Hill Organics

Warm peaches, crumbly crust and ice cream topping -- who doesn't love cobbler?

Serves 8

4 cups of yellow and/or white peaches, wedged

1 tablespoon fresh grated ginger

2 tablespoon of honey

1 cup of butter, cubed and kept cold

1 teaspoon of salt

¾ cup raw sugar

2 cup unbleached all purpose flour

- Preheat the oven at 375F

- In a bowl, toss the peaches with the ginger and honey, spread onto a casserole dish.

- In a food processor, place flour, sugar, butter, salt, pulse until the mixture becomes crumbly.

- Spread flour mixture over the peaches, and bake until the fruits start bubbling on the sides and the crust reaches a perfect golden brown, about 45 minutes.

- Serve with ice cream, crème fraiche or whipped cream

eat this with...
Alta Colina Late Harvest Viognier
Eos Gewurztraminer
Mitchella Riportella Bianco
Red Soles Stiletto

carrot halwa by Nirvana Lounge

Introduced by the traders in Middle East, this dish showcased their fine nuts and the delicate spices. Centuries later an upscale lounge in Beverly Hills (Nirvana) adopted this recipe and made it their own.

Serves 8
- **2 pounds carrots, grated**
- **4 cups milk**
- **2 cups granulated sugar**
- **1 2/3 cup dry powdered milk**
- **1 teaspoon cardamom seeds**
- **3 tablespoons ghee**
- **Optional: Cashews or crushed pistachios for garnish.**

eat this with...
LXV Crimson Jewel

- Place the carrots and milk in a large pot and bring to a boil over medium heat, reduce the heat to medium-low. Cook, stirring frequently until the milk is absorbed into the carrots.

- Add the sugar, dry powdered milk, and cardamom seeds to the pot. Stir everything together and cook for 5 minutes, remove from heat, and set aside.

- In a large frying pan, heat the ghee over high heat, then add the carrot mixture. Cook and stir until the mixture turns a golden brown, remove from heat and serve.

The halwa can be served in bowls, or pressed into a mold to be shaped. Optional: cashews or crushed pistachios can be used as a garnish.

pavlova by Chef Charles D. Paladin Wayne

Pavlova (pav-LOH-vuh) - This meringue crust dessert topped with fresh fruits became very popular in Australia and New Zealand after Russian prima ballerina, Anna Matveyevna Pavlova's visit.

Serves 10

3 egg whites
1 pinch salt
1 cup white sugar
1 tablespoon cornstarch
1 teaspoon lemon juice
1 1/4 cups heavy whipping cream
1/2 cup confectioners' sugar
1 pint fresh fruit

- Preheat oven to 300F. Line a sheet pan with parchment paper. Draw a 9 inch circle on the parchment. An easy way to do this is to draw around the outside of a 9 inch pan with a pencil.

- In a large bowl, beat egg whites on high speed until soft peaks form. Add 3/4 cup of the sugar gradually, while continuing to whip. Make sure sugar is completely dissolved. Mix together the remaining 1/4 cup sugar with the cornstarch; lightly fold into meringue with lemon juice.

- Spread a layer of meringue to fit circle on parchment, approximately 1/4 inch thick. With remainder of mixture, pipe or spoon swirls around the edges to form a shallow bowl shape.

- Bake at 300F for 1 hour. Turn off oven, but leave meringue in oven for an additional 30 minutes. When cool, the meringue should be hard on the outside, and slightly moist on the inside.

- In a large bowl, combine the cream and half a cup of confectioners' sugar, and whip until thickened. Decorate with fruit of your choice; strawberries and kiwis are excellent.

eat this with...
Broken Earth Vin de Vie
Mitchella Riportella Bianco
Paso Port Tawny Port

chapter 6 - desserts

chocolate macadamia soufflé by Ranchita Canyon Vineyards

Teresa Hinrichs makes these chocolate macadamia soufflés to pair with the Ranchita Canyon Dark Secret Petite Sirah "Port". Having both is like a double treat!

Serves 4

½ **cup whole milk**
½ **cup water**
½ **cup powdered sugar**
½ **cup cocoa**
2 **tablespoons flour**
4 **ounces semisweet chocolate, chopped**
2 **egg whites, room temperature**
1 **egg yolk**
1 **pinch of cream of tartar**
4 **tablespoons granulated sugar**
6 **tablespoons chopped macadamia nuts**
Powdered sugar for dusting
Whipped topping or nonfat yogurt

- Preheat oven to 350F. Spray soufflé cups with nonfat cooking spray and set aside.

- In a medium saucepan, combine milk, water and sift in the powdered sugar, cocoa and flour. Stir in the chocolate. Cook on low heat 4-5 minutes, stirring constantly until mixture thickens.

- In a small bowl, beat the egg white and cream of tartar until soft peaks form. Gradually add the sugar and beat until stiff.

- Add the vanilla, egg yolk, and 4 tablespoons chopped macadamia nuts to the cooled chocolate mixture. Fold in the egg whites. Pour into soufflé cups and sprinkle with remaining chopped nuts.

- Bake on cookie sheet 15-20 minutes. Insert a toothpick in the center. Top with a whipped topping or nonfat yogurt and powdered sugar. Serve immediately.

eat this with...
Ranchita Canyon "Port"

chapter 6 - desserts

dark chocolate profiteroles by Chef Andre , Paso Terra Seafood

These little French treats are decadent and not that difficult to make. Impress your guests by serving these for dessert.

Puff Dough
- ½ cup water
- 4 ounces butter
- 4 ounces bread flour
- 1 ounces chocolate powder
- 4 eggs

Cream
- ½ quart milk
- 2 teaspoon vanilla
- 4 egg yolks
- 4 ounces sugar
- 2 ounces flour
- 2 ounces white chocolate

- Preheat oven 375F.

- Bring water, butter to a boil. Add bread flour and chocolate powder. Make a paste and dry over low flame for 3 minutes. Remove and add 4 eggs, one at a time until thoroughly mixed. Pipe on to a greased cookie sheet and bake at until puffs become golden in color (approximately 20 minutes).

- Boil milk with vanilla. Be careful it does not boil over the pan. Mix yolks with sugar with whisk. Add flour and mix. Pour milk into yolk mixture while whisking. Pour into sauce pan and bring to a boil. Place cream in a bowl to cool down.

- Make small hole in puffs and pipe cream into puff. Melt white chocolate and drizzle on puff.

eat this with...
Graveyard Deliverance
Paso Port Ruby Port
Red Soles Sticky Paws
Tablas Creek Vin De Paille

belgian chocolate mousse by Robin's Restaurant

A high quality Belgian chocolate is the secret ingredient in this delicious mousse.

Serves 6
   12 ounces Callebaut (or other Belgian) chocolate
   1/2 cup strongly brewed coffee
   3/4 cup unsalted butter
   6 each eggs, separated
   Pinch salt
   1 pint heavy whipping cream
   1/2 cup sugar

- In a large stainless steel bowl, combine chocolate, coffee and butter. Set bowl over atop a pot of simmering water until chocolate is melted. Remove from the heat and cool slightly. Whisk in egg yolks one at a time to emulsify.

- In a mixer bowl, whisk heavy cream until stiff peaks form. Fold the heavy cream mixer into the chocolate mixture, working in batches.

- Rinse out the mixer bowl and whip egg whites with a pinch of salt until quite stiff. Slowly add sugar into stiff egg whites and whip for another 30 seconds. Fold egg whites into chocolate/cream mixture, working in batches.

- Using a piping bag, or a spoon, fill your desired glasses and let set for 1 hour.

- Garnish with whipped cream and chocolate shavings.

eat this with...
   Clayhouse Old Vines Petite Sirah
   Graveyard Deliverance
   Paso Port Violeta Port
   Pear Valley Bom Final
   Robert Hall Vintage Port

eat this with...
Shale Oak Cabernet Sauvignon

manchego cheesecake by Chef Alexander Martin, Crush Catering

Manchego Cheesecake with Membrillo, Aged Balsamic, Olive Oil
(Chef Alex recommends Olivas de Oro Arbequina Olive Oil)

24 ounces Manchego cheese	3 eggs	4 cups of granulated sugar
24 ounces cream cheese	4 pounds quince, roughly chopped	1 cup balsamic vinegar
6 ounces milk	1 vanilla pod, split	¼ cup honey
1 cup sugar	2 strips of lemon zest	¼ cup olive oil
¾ cup sour cream	3 tablespoons lemon juice	

- For the cheesecake: Cube the cheese into ½ inch chunks and add into blender. Slowly add 6 ounces milk and blend until smooth. Slowly add cream cheese, sugar and blend for 5 minutes on a slow setting. In a separate bowl, mix the flour and eggs. Mix in cheese puree until all ingredients are blended smoothly and add the sour cream. Bake 325F for 15-25 minutes.

- For the membrillo: Place quince pieces in a large saucepan (6-8 quarts) and cover with water. Add the vanilla pod and lemon peel and bring to a boil. Reduce to a simmer, cover, and let cook until the quince pieces are fork tender (30-40 minutes). Strain the water from the quince pieces. Discard the vanilla pod but keep the lemon peel with the quince. Purée the quince pieces in a food processor or blender. Measure the quince purée. Whatever amount of quince purée you have, that's how much sugar you will need. So if you have 4 cups of purée, you'll need 4 cups of sugar. Return the quince purée to the large pan. Heat to medium-low. Add the sugar. Stir with a wooden spoon until the sugar has completely dissolved. Add the lemon juice. Continue to cook over a low heat, stirring occasionally, for 1-1 1/2 hours, until the quince paste is very thick and has a deep orange pink color. Preheat oven to a low 125F. Line a 8x8 baking pan with parchment paper (do not use wax paper, it will melt!). Grease the parchment paper with a thin coating of butter. Pour the cooked quince paste into the parchment paper-lined baking pan. Smooth out the top of the paste so it is even. Place in the oven for about an hour to help it dry. Remove from oven and let cool. To serve, cut into squares or wedges and present with Manchego cheesecake.

- For Aged Balsamic: Stir balsamic vinegar and honey together in a small saucepan and place over high heat. Bring to a boil, reduce heat to low, and simmer until the vinegar mixture has reduced to 1/3 cup, about 10 minutes. Set the balsamic reduction aside to cool.

walnut carrot cake by Limerock Orchards

Limerock Orchards is a 100% family owned and operated Paso Robles walnut company. They take nuts from their 23-acre orchard and produce a delicious walnut oil. This recipe showcases the nut!

Serves 12

Cake
2 cups all purpose flour
2 teaspoons baking soda
1 teaspoon salt
1 teaspoon cinnamon, ground
1 teaspoon dried ginger, ground
2 cup sugar
1 1/4 cup roasted walnut oil
4 eggs
3 cups carrots, peeled and grated
1 1/4 cups coarsely chopped walnuts

Icing
10 ounces cream cheese
5 tablespoons unsalted butter
2 1/2 cups powdered sugar
1/4 cup pure maple syrup
12 walnut halves (for garnish)

eat this with...
Clavo Cellars Petite Sirah
Opolo Zinfandel
Paso Port Angelica White Port
Pomar Junction Amber Moonlight

- Cake Preparation: Preheat oven to 350°F. Line the bottom of two 9" round pans with waxed paper or parchment. Butter and flour paper or parchment, removing excess flour. Whisk flour, baking soda, salt and cinnamon in medium bowl. In a separate bowl, beat sugar and walnut oil until well blended. Add eggs one at a time. Gradually add flour mixture and stir until blended. Stir in carrots, walnuts and ginger. Pour mixture evenly into prepared pans.

- Bake cakes until tester inserted into center comes out clean, about 40 minutes. Cool cakes in pans 10-15 minutes, then turn out onto racks. Peel off waxed paper and cool cakes completely.

- Icing Preparation: Beat cream cheese and butter in large bowl until airy. Add powdered sugar and beat at low speed until combined. Beat in maple syrup. Chill until just firm enough to spread, 30 minutes.

- Place first cake layer on platter. Spread with 3/4 cup icing. Top with second layer. Spread remaining icing over entire cake. Arrange walnut halves around top edge and Serve at room temperature.

chapter 6 - desserts

bittersweet chocolate caramel tart

by Chef Ryan Swarthout

This bittersweet chocolate caramel tart with soft whipped cream is the perfect way to end any meal. While it can certainly be served with a dessert wine, this recipe also pairs nicely with the dry, bold wines of Paso Robles.

Crust
- 1 cup all-purpose flour
- ¼ cup brown sugar, packed
- 2 tablespoons cornstarch
- ¼ teaspoon salt
- ½ cup butter, cut into ½ inch cubes
- 1 tablespoon ice water
- 1 egg yolk

Caramel Layer
- 1 14 ounce can sweetened condensed milk
- ½ cup brown sugar, packed
- 6 tablespoons butter, diced
- 2 tablespoons golden syrup or dark syrup
- 1 teaspoon vanilla extract

Chocolate Glaze
- 6 ounces bittersweet chocolate
- 3 tablespoons heavy cream

- **Crust:** Preheat oven to 350 degrees. Spray a 13x9 cake pan with non-stick spray. Blend flour, sugar, cornstarch and salt in a food processor. Add butter. Pulse the food processor until coarse meal forms. Add ice water and egg yolk. Blend until moist clumps form. Press dough onto bottom (not sides) of pan; pierce all over with fork. Bake until golden about 22 minutes. Cool completely.

- **Caramel Layer:** Whisk milk, sugar, butter, syrup and vanilla in a sauce pan. Heat over medium heat until sugar dissolves, butter melts and mixture comes to a boil. Boil gently until caramel is pale golden and thick, whisking constantly, about 8 minutes. Pour caramel evenly over crust; cool 15 minutes to set.

- **Chocolate Glaze:** Heat chocolate and cream in a small sauce pot over low heat, stirring occasionally until smooth. Do not overheat or chocolate will separate. Spread chocolate over caramel layer; sprinkle with sea salt. Refrigerate until chocolate is set 1 hour. Cut into squares and serve with soft whipped cream.

eat this with...

Eberle Barbera
JUSTIN Obtuse
Penman Springs Cabernet
Roxo Port Paso Melange

mini pecan tarts by Lisa Pretty

These little tarts are perfect for the holidays. The cream cheese pastry is easy to make and melts in your mouth along with the pecan filling. This sweet treat is best enjoyed with a glass of dessert wine. Paso has a wide range of dessert wines available from traditional ports, fortified zinfandel, late harvest viognier and sparkling. Pick your favorite and indulge.

24 mini tarts

Pastry:
8 ounces cream cheese, cut into cubes
1 cup butter, cut into cubes
2 ½ cups all purpose flour

Filling:
5 tablespoons butter
1 cup brown sugar
¾ cup corn syrup
½ teaspoon salt
1 ½ cups chopped pecans
2 teaspoon vanilla extract
3 eggs, beaten
2 tablespoons dark rum
24 pecan halves

eat this with...
Broken Earth Moscato
Halter Ranch Vin de Paille
Pomar Junction Amber Moonlight
Pretty-Smith Tawny Port
Robert Hall Orange Muscat
Rotta Black Monukka

- Preheat oven to 350F.

- Place the pastry ingredients into a food processor and pulse until it resembles corn meal. Remove from food processor and form 24 small balls. Press each ball into the mini tart pan, covering the bottom and sides.

- In a small sauce pan, melt the butter and stir in the brown sugar, syrup, salt and chopped pecans. Stir until the mixture begins to boil and then remove from heat. Stir in the chopped pecans, vanilla. Stir in the egg and dark rum.

- Spoon the filling into the shells and place a pecan half on top of each. Bake in oven for 25-30 minutes or until filling has set.

smore's chocolate tart by Chef Will Torres, Restaurant at JUSTIN

Chef Will has taken a simple childhood treat and turned it into a gourmet delight for adults. The recipe is broken into 3 separate parts that come together for a spectacular dessert.

Serves 8

Graham Cracker Crust
- 1 1/4 cups finely ground graham crackers
- 2 tablespoons granulated sugar
- 4 tablespoons unsalted butter, melted

- Position a rack in the center of the oven and heat the oven to 350°F

- Have an ungreased 9 1/2-inch fluted tart pan with a removable bottom ready.

- In a medium bowl, mix the crumbs and sugar with a fork until well blended.

- Drizzle the melted butter over the crumbs and mix until evenly moistened.

- Put the crumbs in the tart pan (chef likes to use a piece of plastic wrap between his hands and the crust) and use your hands to spread the crumbs so that they cover the bottom of the pan and sides.

- Use your fingers to pinch and press some of the crumbs around the inside edge of the pan to cover the sides evenly and create a wall about a scant 1/4 inch thick.

- Redistribute the remaining crumbs evenly over the bottom of the pan and press firmly to make a compact layer.

- Bake the crust until it smells nutty and fragrant, about 5-10 minutes.

Chocolate Custard
  8 ounces semi sweet chocolate
  6 ounces cream
  2 ounces milk
  2 teaspoons sugar
  1 egg

- ❧ Put chocolate in bowl. Combine cream, milk and sugar in a pot and bring to a boil. Then pour over chocolate. Mix until combined. Whisk in egg. Pour into cooled Graham Cracker Crust.

- ❧ Bake at 300F for 20-25 minutes.

- ❧ Let cool in fridge until set, about 2 hours.

Italian Meringue (Marshmallow Fluff)
  10 1/2 ounces sugar
  2 ounces glucose (or corn syrup)
  4 ounces grams water
  7 ounces grams egg whites

eat this with...
JUSTIN Obtuse

- ❧ In a small saucepan, dissolve the sugar into the glucose and water until it is the texture of wet sand. Cook the mixture until it reaches 240F.

- ❧ In a mixing bowl with a whisk attachment, whisk the egg whites until soft peaks form. Pour the heated sugar mixture into the egg whites in a light steady stream. Continue to whisk on high speed until the side of the bowl is completely cool.

- ❧ After cool, pipe on top of chilled tart and use a torch to bruleé the top.

grandma's espresso-chocolate brownies

by Pam Bowker, Caliza Winery

Pam remembers making these with her Grandmother's watchful eye to ensure that she measured correctly, mixed softly and buttered the pan just so. She has put her own modern-day twist on this old family recipe. This brownie has a soft center and a slight crunch of espresso bean.

Serves 12
- Butter and flour for preparing the pan
- 1/3 cup dark chocolate-covered espresso beans
- 4 ounces (1 stick of butter)
- 2 ounces dark chocolate chips
- 2 large eggs
- 1 cup granulated sugar
- 1 tablespoon cocoa (unsweetened)
- 1 teaspoon vanilla extract
- ¼ cup unbleached all-purpose flour
- Confectioners' sugar, for dusting
- Red raspberries, for garnish (optional)
- Whipped cream, for garnish (optional)

- ∾ Preheat oven to 350°. Butter a 9-inch square baking pan, then line the base with parchment paper. Butter the paper, then dust with flour. Pulse the chocolate-covered espresso beans in a food processor to a coarse powder and set aside.

- ∾ Melt the butter and chocolate chips in the top of a double boiler set over simmering water, stirring frequently, until melted. Stir in the cocoa powder until combined. Remove from the heat.

- ∾ In a medium mixing bowl, beat the eggs and sugar together until pale and lemon-colored. Add the vanilla.

- ∾ Fold in the chocolate mixture, stirring just until blended—do not over mix. Sift the flour and fold it gently into batter. Fold in the ground espresso beans. Scoop into the prepared pan and bake for 20 to 25 minutes, until the center is set. (Do not over-bake.) Cool in the pan for 30 minutes, then cutting into squares. Dust with confectioners' sugar. If desired, garnish with a jumble of raspberries and serve with a dollop of whipped cream.

eat this with...

Caliza Syrah

molten chocolate cakes by Chef Jeff Wiesinger, Jeffrys Catering

The cakes should be served warm with a soft and gooey middle!
Chef Jeff makes these cakes for a large number of wine events
-- there are never any leftovers.

Serves 8

9 ounces bittersweet chocolate, chopped
2 sticks (1 cup) unsalted butter
4 eggs
4 egg yolks
1/2 cup granulated sugar
2 tablespoons all purpose flour
Pan coating spray, as needed
8 fresh strawberries, sliced for garnish
Powdered sugar, 1 tablespoon

eat this with...
Graveyard Deliverance
Opolo Late Harvest Zinfandel
Red Soles Sticky Paws
Robert Hall Vintage Port

- Preheat oven to 400 degrees.

- Spray 8, 4-6 ounce ramekins or muffin cups with pan coating.

- Melt chocolate & butter in a double boiler. Stir until completely melted & combined; Set aside to cool slightly.

- In a large bowl combine eggs & egg yolks, whisk until frothy. Add sugar and continue to whisk together until mixture has doubled in volume than whisk in the flour. Slowly add the melted chocolate mixture to the egg mixture & stir until combined. Divide the batter among the coated ramekins and place ramekins on a sheet pan.

- Bake until the sides of the cakes are set but the center remains soft, about 11-14 minutes. Carefully remove cakes from the oven & invert cakes onto plates.

- Garnish the cakes with fresh sliced strawberries & powdered sugar.

Menus

Entertain your guests with a menu paired with Paso Robles wine. Here are a number of creative pairings from a diverse group of chefs - try one for your next special get together.

BROKEN EARTH WINERY

Dinner Down Under
by Chef Charles D. Paladin Wayne

Chef Charlie's menu paired with Broken Earth wines is inspired by Australian cuisine. Invite your best mates when you try these recipes. Serve each course and you will be "full as a goog"!

Prawn and Scallop Pie p46
Broken Earth Reserve Petit Verdot

Salad of Field Mache with Pancetta Crisp
and Candied Garlic,Baby Heirloom Tomatoes,
Sheep's Feta and Banyuls Sherry Vinaigrette p75
Quadrant Gold (Viognier, Chardonnay, Pinot Gris, Albarino)

Roast Leg of Lamb p144
Seasoned with Garlic, Mustard, Mint and Rosemary
Served with Crushed Kumara, Sauté of Canelinni Beans,
Roast Red Pepper and Sugar Snap Peas
Broken Earth Merlot

Pavlova p165
Broken Earth Vin de Vie

Broken Earth Winery is a customer-focused team proudly representing Paso Robles. They produce unique wines that are estate grown, harvested & bottled in Paso Robles. The wines reflect winemaker Chris Cameron's committed & passionate approach to all aspects of winemaking. Structure & balance are most critical; each varietal released is an accurate reflection of the style & the region. The grapes are sustainably (Certified California Sustainable Vineyard) farmed on its own 2,500 acre property originally planted with 522 acres in 1973. The winery is 100% solar powered, with a commitment to sustainable winemaking practices. Broken Earth Winery remains committed to sustainable ideals, and to continuing to bolster the high-quality reputation of Paso Robles wines.

The Broken Earth tasting room is a great place to browse for unique gifts and food items. While you're there ask about getting your own personalized wine label. Broken Earth's design team will create a wine label tailored to fit your vision. This kind of gift is great for any special person, occasion or celebration.

Open Daily 10:30am - 5:30pm
5625 Highway 46 East, Paso Robles
805.239.2562   brokenearthwinery.com

Vineyard Luncheon
by Brigit Binns

This menu was created for a number of charitable auction lots hosted by Caliza. There is nothing better than a walk in the vineyard, discovering a set table hidden amongst the vines ready to enjoy a leisurely luncheon shared with friends old and new.

Platter of Home-made Calamata Hummus p15,
Assorted Salumi, and Local Sheep's Cheese
Caliza Pink

Mixed Shellfish and Couscous Salad
with Meyer Lemon Vinaigrette p73
Caliza Kissin' Cousins
(Viognier, Grenache Blanc and Roussanne)

Grilled Game Hens Provencal p102
with Grilled Fingerling Potatoes and Asparagus
Caliza Azimuth (Grenache, Syrah and Mourvedre)

Grandma's Espresso-Chocolate Brownies p181
with Fresh Seasonal Berries
Caliza Syrah

Caliza is

…Spanish for the word 'limestone'.
…dedication to the pursuit of perfection.
…an ongoing dream fulfilled one day at a time.
…respect for the earth, mankind and tradition.
…cutting edge wines with new wine making styles.

The dream may have begun in the Tuscan countryside of Italy, however, the pursuit to find the perfect vineyard was realized when discovering Paso Robles. In 2003, Carl and Pam Bowker purchased their small hillside vineyard on the west side of Paso in the Templeton Gap. After much research they planted mostly Rhône style varietals along with a little Primitivo and Tempranillo. With the first release in 2006, Caliza is "one of the newest players in west Paso" producing an impressive list of small hand-crafted lots of red and white Rhône style blends. You will often find Carl and Pam behind the bar in their den like tasting room talking about wine and the vineyard.

Open Thursday-Sunday 11am - 4:30pm
or by appointment
2570 Anderson Road, Paso Robles
805.237.1480   calizawinery.com

CASS
Vineyard & Winery

From Garden to Table
by Chef Jacob Lovejoy

When you visit the Cass tasting room you will likely notice the lush vegetable garden. Chef Jacob cares for the garden with his green thumb and uses the bounty of his harvest in the Cass Café.

Tomato Confit. Japanese eggplant crisp, buffalo bocconcini p36
Cass Rosé

Mano de Leon scallop. Meyer lemon and chili pistou, spicy micro-greens p45
Cass Viognier

Puree of Fagioli bean soup.
Pancetta lardon, Parmesan crisp p87
Cass Grenache

Chicken Saltimboca 104
Cass Rockin' One Red

The Cass Tasting Room is a "stunning contemporary winery" said Tribune Wine writer Janis Switzer, and she was right. The fact that it houses some of Paso Robles finest and most touted Rhone wines makes Cass Winery a must on any wine country tour.

The Tasting Room opened its doors to the public in 2005 offering wine lovers a comprehensive Tasting Room where the wines could be showcased, sampled and purchased.

In addition, a gourmet food menu, prepared by Chef Jacob Lovejoy, allows you to pair your wines with cheeses and other seasonal offerings, which can be enjoyed out on the veranda or in the light and bright Tasting Room itself.

Open Daily 11am-5pm
7350 Linne Road, Paso Robles
805.239.1730   casswines.com

CELLARS

French Picnic

by Chef Laurent Grangien, Bistro Laurent

There is nothing like a leisurely French lunch complete with wine pairings. Try this menu for your next picnic.

Chilled Pea Soup p82
Clavo Grenache Blanc

Steak Tartare p40
Clavo Collusion (Bordeaux Blend)

Niçoise Salad Sandwich p44
Clavo Enigma (Proprietary Blend)

Clavo Cellars specializes in hand-grown artisan wines that express the character and culture of Paso Robles.

Under the guidance of veteran winegrower and winemaker, Neil Roberts, Clavo focuses on varietals that excel amid some of the region's most notable vineyards.

The name Clavo means "nail" in Spanish – a play on Neil's name. He acquired this nickname early in his career as a viticulturist, as given to him by Mexican-American vineyard workers. It was a form of acceptance, as well as an invitation into their world. Clavo wines are dedicated to these people and all who have inspired Neil along the way.

The resulting wines are made to express the pure personality of the vineyard, as guided by Neil's hand. These wines are offered in a spirit of approachability and enjoyment, embracing the casual elegance for which the Central Coast is renowned.

Open Daily 12 - 5pm
315 South Main Street, Templeton
805.226.0174   clavocellars.com

Clayhouse
WINES

Decadent Lunch
by Robin's Restaurant

Robin's Restaurant, located in the charming town of Cambria, is known for inspiring menus with handcrafted global cuisine. Try this lunch menu paired with Clayhouse wines for a decadent lunch the next time you are entertaining.

Heirloom Tomato & Fresh Mozzarella Salad
with Walnut Vinaigrette p62
Clayhouse Adobe White

Lamb Kefta Sliders with Blue Cheese p31
Clayhouse Vineyard Malbec

Belgium Chocolate Mousse p169
Clayhouse Old Vines Petite Sirah

Each offering is carefully crafted from select grapes, hand-picked from small vineyard blocks that over the years have proven their ability to produce exciting wines. The result? A refined, well-balanced wine, with elegant textures and flavors; wine that clearly expresses the varietal, while reflecting the distinctive appeal of Paso Robles.

The 150-year-old adobe structure -- the Clayhouse itself -- really is the ideal symbol for the vineyards. Like the adobe, the wines are created from the earth, cultivated by hand, and nurtured by family traditions. For the Middleton family, those traditions and deep passion for agricultural businesses go back more than four generations. Today, Clayhouse extends that proud legacy with its selection of exceptional wines, all hand-crafted in a refined, elegant style that reflects the unique character of Paso Robles. All the fruit comes from the estate Red Cedar vineyard on the outskirts of Paso Robles.

Open Wednesday - Sunday 12– 6pm
Monday & Tuesday by appointment only
849 13th Street, Paso Robles
805.238.7055   clayhousewines.com

GRAVEYARD

VINEYARDS

Harvest Feast
By Chef Andre Averseng, Paso Terra Seafood

Although Chef Andre specializes in seafood at his restaurant located in downtown Paso Robles, his multi talents as a true French chef are clearly demonstrated in this menu. Created as a harvest celebration, each course is paired perfectly with a Graveyard Vineyard wine. Bon appétit!

Oyster Saffron Chowder p91
Graveyard Chardonnay

Spicy Shrimp Romesco on a bed of Spaghetti Squash 41
Graveyard Tempranillo "Spanish Castle Magic"

Swordfish Wrapped with Prosciutto p97
on Purple Potatoes with Syrah Reduction
Graveyard Estate Syrah

Skirt Steak Roule with Wild Mushroom and
Wine Reduction sauce on Rosemary infused Polenta p149
Graveyard Petite Syrah "Dark Phantom"

Dark Chocolate Profiteroles with Vanilla Cream,
topped with White Chocolate Drizzle p167
Graveyard Chocolate Dessert Wine "Deliverance"

Graveyard Vineyards is a small family winery owned by Rob and Paula Campbell-Taylor. Located above the historic Pleasant Valley Cemetery, just 6 minutes from Highway 46 East and Airport Road, the winery is so warm and welcoming you will feel like you are visiting an old friend on your very first visit.

The award winning wines like the Sauvignon Blanc, Paso Tombstone White, Paso Tombstone Pink, Paso Tombstone Red, Mortal Zin, Dark Phantom & Deliverance are priced for everyday enjoyment. Or as the owners say they are priced to allow you to "Drink in Peace".

The views from the hilltop winery are breathtaking with plenty of room for picnicking, fishing in the pond & enjoying a stroll through the vineyards.

Open Thursday-Monday 11am-5pm
6994 Estrella Road, San Miguel
805.467.2043   GraveyardVineyards.com

J.LOHR
VINEYARDS & WINES

J.LOHR
VINEYARDS & WINES

A Taste of Italy
by Il Cortile Ristorante

Located in downtown Paso Robles, Il Cortile is known for fine Italian dining. They have provided this menu of classic dishes to bring a taste of Italy to your table. Each dish has been paired with a J. Lohr wine -- invite your friends, open a bottle, and start cooking. The aromas of the hearty dishes will fill your home.

Sausage & Cannelli Beans p114
J. Lohr Estates South Ridge Syrah

Mushroom Risotto p34
J. Lohr Highlands Bench Pinot Noir

Braised Lamb Shank p145
J. Lohr Hilltop Cabernet Sauvignon

Four decades ago, Jerry Lohr became one of a handful of early pioneers to explore the potential for premium winegrowing on California's Central Coast. In the late 1960s, he began searching for the ideal location to plant a vineyard. Raised on a farm, Jerry understood the importance of climate, soil quality and location. His instincts led him to the Central Coast, a unique region with one of California's longest growing seasons. Selecting Monterey County's Arroyo Seco appellation for his original vineyard, Jerry planted his first 280 acres of grapes beginning in 1972. Ideally suited for cool-climate winegrowing, these vineyards have become an acclaimed source for Chardonnay, Riesling, Valdiguié and Pinot Noir.

Taking a lesson from the winegrowing regions of Burgundy and Bordeaux, Jerry understood that great Chardonnay and Cabernet Sauvignon could not be grown side-by-side. He, then, began planting Cabernet Sauvignon, Merlot and other red varietals in the Paso Robles region in 1988. Today J. Lohr Vineyards & Wines includes more than 1,300 acres of vineyards in Monterey County, approximately 2,300 acres in Paso Robles, and 35 acres in Napa Valley.

Open Daily 10am-5pm
6169 Airport Road, Paso Robles
(805) 239-8900   jlohr.com

JUSTIN

Steak Night
by Chef Will Torres

The Restaurant at JUSTIN offers guests the ultimate food & wine experience with world class service. Guests sit back and relax as Executive Chef Will Torres artfully transforms local ingredients into unparalleled cuisine. Chef Will created this menu so that those who like to dine at home can bring a touch of JUSTIN to their table.

Butter Leaf Salad p61
JUSTIN Sauvignon Blanc

Grilled Charter Oak Striploin p146
JUSTIN ISOSCELES

Smores Chocolate Tart p178
JUSTIN OBTUSE

Mission Statement: *"To belong in the company of the finest wines in the world."*

JUSTIN Vineyards & Winery was founded in 1981 and is known for crafting world class wines that reflect the unique soils and climate of its Paso Robles property. Emphasis is placed on making Bordeaux-style blends and single varietals, combining Old World tradition with New World techniques.

The property at JUSTIN features a tasting room, luxury suite accommodations and a restaurant – making it the only winery on the Central Coast to offer all three options.

Designed to maximize the beatuiful vineyard views and showcase award winning wines, the Tasting Room at JUSTIN Vineyards & Winery provides the perfect setting to learn about and taste JUSTIN wines.

Open Daily 10am - 4:30pm
11680 Chimney Rock Road, Paso Robles
805-238-6932   JUSTINwine.com

Indian Royal *Dawaat*
by Neeta Mittal

The history of Indian food tells us that European invaders considered it closely to what Gods thought of ambrosia: delightful, heavenly and delicate, often indulging in dawaats - a Royal Indian feast. Bring a taste of India to your table with this menu paired with LXV wine.

Tandoori Chicken p29
LXV Viognier Summer Satine

Chicken Biryani p113
LXV Heart Note

Mutton Curry p137
LXV Rising Tempo

Carrot Halwa p164
LXV Crimson Jewel

Romantic evenings have moved from being a deux to ménage-a trois: you, them and a bottle of wine. LXV Wine, inspired by the 64 arts of KamaSutra, aspires to elevate those romantic moments.

LXV has emerged from the teaming up of two entrepreneurial geniuses – those of Kunal and Neeta Mittal. And the talented iconoclastic winemaker Amy Butler. The style of the wine is at once classic and contemporary, showcasing the uniqueness of Paso Robles AVA.

The anchor of each label is the portrait of an artist and their philosophy on art and sensuality. "Sensuality involves more than the use of the five traditional senses; with awareness and intuition, it goes beyond just sensing" explains founder Neeta Mittal, who is a dancer, choreographer and an award-winning filmmaker.

The Mittals have created a sensory tasting room in downtown Paso Robles, paying a subtle tribute to their heritage. They also host private tastings with Indian flair, in their eclectic barn.

A highly customized modern bar, plush day beds, and their warm Indian hospitality awaits you...

Open Thursday-Tuesday 1 - 7pm
1306B Pine Street, Paso Robles
805.296.1902   lxvwine.com

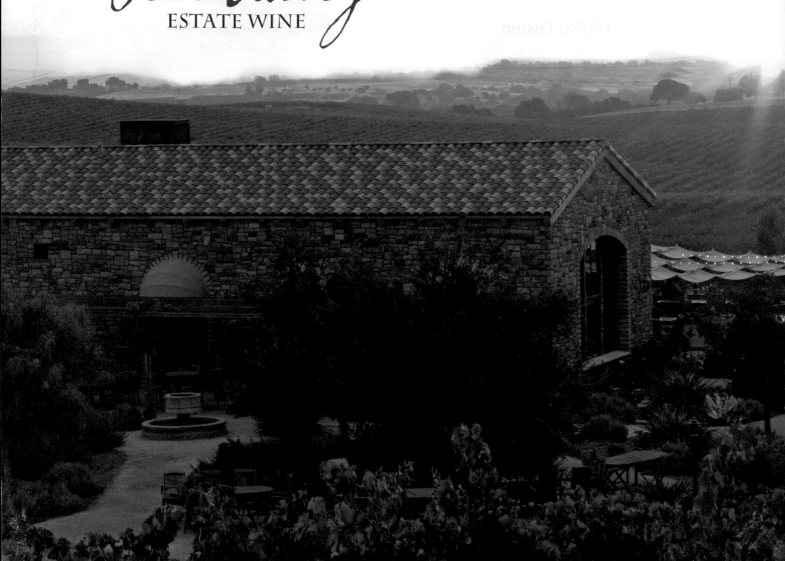

Pear Valley
ESTATE WINE

Global Fusion
By Chef Thomas Drahos, Avant-Garde Catering

Chef Thomas has created a globally inspired menu with each of the five courses paired with one of Pear Valley's limited production wines. Take your taste buds on a trip around the globe with this menu.

Black pepper calamari with sweet and spicy sauce p25
Pear Valley Frizzante Muscat

Pan seared local black cod, smoked grapes,
salsify bur blanc, flambéed bay scallops p52
Pear Valley Albariño

Chicken Vindaloo p111
Pear Valley Charbono

Pork Puttanesca p133
Pear Valley Aglianico

Baked plums, honey glazed puffed rice,
vanilla whipped cream, and chocolate gel
Pear Valley Belle Fin

Pear Valley is Tom and Kathleen Maas' family winery designed to make visitors feel welcome.

Selecting from 24 grape varietals grown on their estate vineyards, they create unique vintages that reflect the vibrant fruit nourished by ancient soils while leaving little impact on the environment. All three of Pear Valley's estate vineyards have been certified Sustainable in Practice (SIP).

The Maas family cordially offers novice wine drinkers, enthusiasts and connoisseurs a taste of the naturally good life captured in each bottle of Pear Valley wine. The diverse offering ranges from dry to sweet, crisp to round, and medium bodied to bold.

Visit the tasting room and enjoy the 360 degree views of Paso Robles countryside while sipping Pear Valley wine. Bring a picnic, sit back and relax while enjoying the soft music piped throughout the picnic area.

Open Daily 11am - 5pm
4900 Union Road, Paso Robles
805.237.2861   pearvalley.com

PENMAN SPRINGS VINEYARD

American Cuisine with a French Twist
by Chef Ryan Swarthout

Crab Cakes with Papaya Slaw
and Sweet Thai Chili Sauce p49
Penman Springs Rosé

Pan Roasted Duck Breast with
Wild Mushroom Risotto and Dried Cherry Sauce p116
Penman Springs Syrah

Braised Short Ribs With Creamy Polenta p155
Penman Springs Meritage

Bittersweet Chocolate Caramel Tart
with Soft Whipped Cream p175
Penman Springs Cabernet Sauvignon

Taste the Art
PENMAN SPRINGS VINEYARD

Penman Springs Vineyard is a family-owned, artisan winery situated in the rolling hills east of Paso Robles. The proprietors, Carl and Beth McCasland, along with winemaker Larry Roberts, craft a lineup of varietal offerings of Muscat Blanc, Merlot, Cabernet Sauvignon, Syrah and Petite Sirah, along with Petit Verdot for use in their "Meritage" blend.

The McCaslands refer to their 40-plus acres as a "garden" and the magic of Penman Springs starts in the vineyard. The grapes enjoy optimum growing conditions of warm days, cool nights, and perfect soils. Add to that a variety of trellis systems — the Smart-Dyson, the open lyre, and the Geneva Double Curtain — and you've got the beginnings of deeply colored, full-bodied wines with rich, balanced flavors.

Stop by for a visit!

Open Thursday-Sunday 11am-5pm
1985 Penman Springs Road, Paso Robles
805.237.7959   penmansprings.com

POMAR JUNCTION
VINEYARD & WINERY

A Dinner of Classics
by Chef Natalie Dorris

Enjoy this all star, classic line-up of menu items on your next get together. The classics really are timeless!

Bay Shrimp Cocktail with Mango and Pineapple p23
Pomar Junction Vineyard Picnic Chardonnay

Niçoise Salad with Seared Ahi p77
Pomar Junction Vineyard Brooster

Pan Roasted Ribeye Steak with
caramelized onions and Blue cheese compound butter p150
Pomar Junction Vineyard Merlot

Owned and operated by the Merrill Family, Pomar Junction Vineyard & Winery showcases eight generations of Central Coast farming through deeply characterful estate wines. With a rich heritage of sustainable practices in the vineyard and minimal intervention in the cellar, Pomar Junction guides estate fruit from vine to glass with a narrow focus on purity of flavor and varietal integrity. After nearly 30 years of growing grapes for many of the finest wineries in California, ranging from ultra premium small producers to the largest international brands, the Merrill's decided to produce their own wines. In addition to the family estate, the finest blocks of grapes from Santa Barbara and Monterey Counties are selected from vineyards managed by a sister firm, Mesa Vineyard Management, Inc. All wines produced are exclusively farmed by the Merrills who believe that control from planting and pruning through harvest, fermentation and cellaring is critical for success. It also ensure a uniform dedication to sustainability, which led our recent Certification to the SIP program within the Central Coast Vineyard Team. The winery name refers to the Merrill Family's concurrent lineage of railroad engineers as well as to bygone days when the Southern Pacific Railroad was responsible for the development of the picturesque Central Coast.

Open Daily from 11am - 5pm
5036 S. El Pomar Road in Templeton
(805) 238-9940   PomarJunction.com

PRETTY  SMITH

Vineyards & Winery

Sunday Supper
by Lisa Pretty

Sometimes it is nice to create a menu of simple, comfort food and enjoy the company of friends. Maybe even play a round of Scrabble over another glass of wine.

French Onion Soup p89
Pretty-Smith Palette de Rouge

Turkey loaf p118 with mashed potatoes
Mission View Cabernet Sauvignon

Mini Pecan Tarts p177
Pretty-Smith Port

Pretty-Smith Vineyards & Winery produces 100% estate-grown fruit under the Pretty-Smith label. The line-up includes a number of stand alone Bordeaux varietals as well as the signature wine, a blend known as Palette de Rouge. The red wines are aged in oak for 3.5 years and bottle aged for an additional year prior to release to create a SOFT, SMOOTH and SILKY style.

The estate property offers wonderful views of the surrounding vineyards and the hills of San Miguel.

With advanced group reservations, the Pretty Café may be booked for food & wine pairing experiences.

Kokopelli awaits!

Open by appointment only
13350 River Road, San Miguel
805.467.3104   PrettySmith.com

Ranchita Canyon
VINEYARD

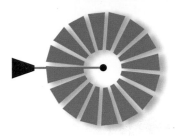

Ranchita Canyon
VINEYARD

Dinner with Friends
by Teresa Hinrichs

This menu paired with Ranchita Canyon wines is ideal for sharing with your friends. Teresa's recipes are perfect for an evening dining on the deck while sipping wine and visiting with guests.

Prosciutto Crostini p27
Ranchita Canyon Cabernet Pfeffer

Teriyaki Flank Steak p129
Ranchita Canyon Cabernet Franc

Chocolate Macadamia Soufflé p166
Ranchita Canyon Dark Secret Petite Sirah "Port"

Ranchita Canyon Vineyard is nestled among the hills overlooking the beautiful countryside. Bill and Teresa Hinrichs came to Paso Robles in 1999 resurrecting the winery that was established in the late 1970's and the vineyard that was planted in the early 1970's.

There are eleven different varietals planted, making wine for every occasion. Come inside the tasting room and enjoy the views while sipping award winning estate wines. Bring a picnic lunch to enjoy on the patio.

Visit Ranchita Canyon Vineyard and enjoy the beauty, serenity and delicious wines.

Open Thursday-Monday 11am-5pm
or by appointment
3439 Ranchita Canyon Road, San Miguel
805.467.9448 ranchitacanyonvineyard.com

~213~

RED SOLES
WINERY

Middle Eastern Fare
by Chef Julie Simon, Thomas Hill Organics

Thomas Hill Organics, located in downtown Paso Robles, is a bistro and wine lounge dedicated to serving creative, fresh food, highlighting the local wines. This middle eastern inspired menu by Chef Julie brings together three tasty courses paired with Red Soles wine. This menu is perfect for lunch or a light dinner.

Greek Salad p63
Red Soles Loose Laces Rosé

Pork Kebabs p128 with Tabbouleh Salad p70
Red Soles Estate Zinfandel

Peach Cobbler p163
Red Soles Stiletto

Red Soles Winery is a small, family owned and operated winery founded by Randy and Cheryl Phillips in March of 2007. Red Soles Winery has proven a natural extension of the farming company that the two have owned since 1991 when they first began growing grapes.

After years of wanting to experiment with their own fruit, Cheryl eventually convinced Randy to make some wine. Not having any equipment, the pair crushed that historic first barrel with their own feet. Following a fruitful romp in that first bin of grapes, Randy and Cheryl stumbled upon the name Red Soles while admiring each other's red, grape stained feet.

Today, the winery boasts over 20 wines, covering an impressive range of whites, reds, roses', and dessert wines. Each wine in their line up is Estate grown, and the duo is proud of the fact that they do not source their wine grapes from any vineyard other than their own.

There is something extremely satisfying about being able to be part of a wine grape's journey from dust to vine and vine to barrel.

Open Daily 11am-5pm
3230 Oakdale Road, Paso Robles
805.226.9898   redsoleswinery.com

ROBERT HALL WINERY

Grilling with Ian McPhee

McPhee's Grill in Templeton has paired up with Robert Hall Winery in this gourmet four course menu. Invite your friends, fire up the grill and create Ian's recipes at home -- each course pairs perfectly with Robert Hall wines.

Grilled Goat Cheese Stuffed fresh Figs wrapped in prosciutto p13
Robert Hall Grenache Blanc

Jambalaya Pasta p54
Robert Hall Chardonnay

Grilled Lamb Chops with roasted red grape zinfandel sauce p141
Robert Hall Zinfandel

Duck Breast with plum poblano chutney p115
Robert Hall Cabernet Sauvignon

"The Essence of Paso Robles"™

Winemaker, Don Brady, has been making food-friendly, age-worthy wines to showcase the finest grapes in Paso Robles since the winery opened in 2001.

The 300 acres of estate fruit deliver 21 different grape varietals, all certified Sustainable in Practice (SIP). The wide range of grapes enable the winery to delivery something for every palate -- including crisp whites, robust reds, unique blends and sweet dessert wines.

On your next trip to Paso Robles be sure to stop by the hospitality center where the knowledgeable and friendly staff will be delighted to provide an exceptional wine tasting experience including a tour of the large wine cavern and production facility. Bring your glass along since there may just be an opportunity for a little barrel sampling.

Picnic facilities and bocce ball courts are also available -- bring a lunch and visit awhile.

Open Daily
Summer 10-6pm Winter 10-5pm
3443 Mill Road, Paso Robles
805.239.1616   roberthallwinery.com

SHALE OAK

A Touch of Spain
by Chef Alexander Martin, Crush Catering

Chef Alex specializes in innovative wine country cuisine. His creativity shines through in this spectacular menu paired with Shale Oak wine. Enjoy!

Prosciutto wrapped Peaches with Blue Cheese,
Red Wine Gastrique, Toasted Pepitas, Garden Pea Shoots p10
Shale Oak Zinfandel

Award Winning Harvest Paella with Kalua Pork,
Caramelized Fennel, Vibrant Cauliflower,
Blistered Peppers, Sylvetta Arugula p125
Shale Oak Petite Sirah

Manchego Cheesecake with Membrillo,
Aged Balsamic, Olivas De Oro Arbequina Olive Oil p171
Shale Oak Cabernet Sauvignon

With a keen eye on sustainability in every facet of their business, and adhering to the belief that form follows function, Shale Oak Winery was built by a carefully crafted team. While each individual is a strong expert in her/his respective field, the group was able to synergistically come together to plan, plant and build a vineyard, winery and tasting room that would have next to zero impact on the surrounding environment.

Two vineyards, totaling a little over 70 acres, are both farmed using sustainable practices, with careful attention paid to energy efficiency, water cleanliness and conservation, safe pest management and wild habitat preservation. Shale Oak Winery produces varietals that grow best in Paso Robles; Cabernet Sauvignon, Syrah, Zinfandel, Petite Sirah, Petit Verdot, Albariño, Viognier and Pinot Gris.

The Gold LEED Certified Tasting Room opened in October 2011, as a showcase for the limited-production, high-quality wines; the result of a holistic vision.

Open Thursday-Monday, 11am-5pm
3235 Oakdale Road
805.239.4800   shaleoakwinery.com

~219~

 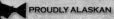
23364

SINCE 2010

SIMPLY INCREDIBLE

FRESH, WILD AND PROUDLY ALASKAN

Wild About Salmon by Keri Scaggs

When you are wild about salmon it is easy to come up with several recipes showcasing this delicious fish. This menu is perfect for parties. Open the Paso wine and let the celebration begin!

Smoked Salmon Mini Toasts p26
Steinbeck Viognier

Smoked Salmon Dip p12
Penman Springs Rosé

Simply Incredible Pizza with Smoked Salmon & Apples p22
Pear Valley Grenache

Guilt-Free BLT p50
Robert Hall Merlot

Simply Incredible was established in 2010 with one goal in mind--to create the very best smoked Alaska wild salmon. Recently the product line has been expanded to include award-winning bacon and chorizo.

The premium sockeye salmon comes from Copper River. Simply Incredible salmon is processed in Alaska's only open-flame smoker using a select mixture of local birch and grape vines from Paso Robles. You'll discover this to be a perfect pairing with the region's wines.

Simply Incredible has offices in Alaska and California -- all products are shipped by overnight express.

Visit SimplyIncredible.com
or call
1-855-772-5666 (855-7-SALMON)

TABLAS
CREEK
VINEYARD

TABLAS CREEK
VINEYARD

A Course for Every Season

Spring: Provencal fish with fennel and white wine p51
Tablas Creek Cotes de Tablas Blanc

Summer: Gazpacho p83
Tablas Creek Rosé

Fall: Pork loin with apricots 127
Tablas Creek Cotes de Tablas

Winter: Braised short ribs with olives p153
Tablas Creek Esprit de Beaucastel

Tablas Creek Vineyard is, at its roots, the story of a friendship between two of the international wine community's leading families: the Perrin family of Château de Beaucastel and the Haas family, American importers, distributors, and retailers since the 19th century. After decades of working together as importer and producer, they decided that California's Mediterranean climate was perfect for the traditional Rhone grapes grown on the Perrins' celebrated estate in Chateauneuf-du-Pape and purchased a 120-acre former cattle ranch in the limestone hills of west Paso Robles.

Planted with vines imported from Beaucastel, Tablas Creek produces estate grown, organically farmed Rhone varieties and Rhone-style blends including Esprit de Beaucastel, Cotes de Tablas and Patelin de Tablas, as well as a selection of varietal wines. In all cases, the winemaking is tailored to maximize the expression of the property's soils, with wines noted for their elegance, their balance, and their friendliness with the clean, bright flavors of the Mediterranean.

Open Daily 10am - 5pm
9339 Adelaida Road, Paso Robles
805.237.1231   tablascreek.com

A Note from the Author

I hope that you have enjoyed this second edition of Eat This With Paso Robles Wine. I truly loved working on the project -- after all it involved three of may favorite things: wine, food and Paso Robles.

The wineries and local chefs made this book extra rewarding. As always, I am amazed by the friendly and helpful attitude of the Paso wine and food industry. I discovered some new wines, many new recipes and even managed to make a few new friends.

If you are interested in following my exploration of food and wine please visit my blog eatthiswith.com.

Lisa Pretty